D0901810

PRAISE FOR
TODAY WE WIN

"In my teens, I had such a strong sense I was born for something special. Then, the realities of adulting set in. My dreams took a backseat to paying the bills and caring for everyone else's needs. Pretty soon, I woke up to a mediocre life that sucked the optimism right out of me. This, my friends, is the book I wish I would have had back then. It's a practical system for stepping into the life you once dreamed about. We have one life to live, a divine destiny, and this book is a key tool to stepping into that!"

– Angie Taylor,
Cofounder and Head of School,
Valor Global Online

"When you define what winning looks like and follow a proven system to get there, you become an unstoppable kingdom-building force. This book is that system."

– **Rohn Gibson**,
Cofounder of ChurchSpring
and Mentor at RohnGibson.com

"When it comes to winning, you need to know the game, the rules, and have a plan. Jordan gives you key elements to win in every area of your life. If you want to grow, this book is a must read."

– **Jeremy D. Brown**,
Cofounder of StoryWay,
CEO Throne Publishing Group,
and bestselling author

TODAY WE WIN

TODAY WE WIN

A SIMPLE SYSTEM TO ACHIEVE
WHAT MATTERS MOST

JORDAN LOFTIS

STORY CHORUS

STORY ⫴ CHORUS

StoryChorus.com
Copyright © 2020 Jordan Loftis
Published by Story Chorus

ISBN 978-1-7344222-0-7

Unless otherwise noted, Scripture quotations are from The ESV® Bible (The Holy Bible, English Standard Version®), copyright © 2001 by Crossway, a publishing ministry of Good News Publishers. Used by permission. All rights reserved.

Cover Photo: Lea Black Photography

TO • DAY \ tə-'dā \

    : the present day, time, or age

WE \'wē \

    : I and the rest of a group that includes me

    : you and I

    : you and I and another or others

WIN \'win \

    : to obtain by work

    : to gain in or as if in battle or contest

    : to succeed in arriving at a place or a state

DEDICATION

To Joelle,
Thank you for taking the leap.
Today, I follow.

TABLE OF CONTENTS

FOREWORD

The first time I met Jordan, he was a hot mess. He was fresh off the heels of a difficult business season and interviewing with the firm where I was a Vice President, and would be his boss. His startup had hit some trouble and we'd stepped in at the eleventh hour to acquire them.

So how did a guy who had no idea what he was doing start a thriving business, build a massive online ministry, launch a podcast with thousands of listeners, and ghostwrite over 30 books since our first encounter less than five years ago?

Because he's driven to make an eternal impact and has more hustle than is normally found in a single person.

In that conference room, I saw incredible talent, desire to be the best version of himself, and the opportunity to grow beyond what he even realized was possible. And he's pushed those of us around him to do the same.

I have a saying that I don't take financial advice from poor people. I also don't take personal development advice from people who haven't exponentially grown themselves. However, I take advice from Jordan, because he's done it, is still doing it, and wrote this book to show you how. It is a byproduct of the pain Jordan and Joelle, his wife, have experienced and conquered.

To me, Jordan's story resembles Dave Ramsey's. Ramsey was once bankrupt and now helps millions escape the shackles of debt. I see Jordan in a similar light, fighting through pain to develop a system to elevate himself, his family, and now everyone who will follow.

This is a guide that removes the guesswork from defining and finding success.

This is a book based on Biblical truths, and grounded in God's word.

This is a system to apply those truths to our lives. It's a reflection of our Father, because we can't win without him.

Satan doesn't want you to implement a system like this. He doesn't want you to be focused and purposeful. He wants you to wake up every day clueless and distracted.

Eternity matters. And as Jordan explains, at the end of the day, our eternal impact on others is how winning is defined. It's not about the cars, the jets, the money... It's about laying up treasures in Heaven. When you define what winning looks like and follow a proven system to get there, you become an unstoppable kingdom-building force.

If you share these beliefs, hopes, and desires, this book is for you.

Rohn Gibson
Cofounder of ChurchSpring
and Mentor at RohnGibson.com

PART ONE:
GIFTS

Our purpose is most powerful when it starts with this question: "If my life became a gift to those around me, what would it be?"

•••

"Let each of you look not only to his own interests, but also to the interests of others."
Philippians 2:4

CHAPTER ONE:

WINNERS
AND
LOSERS

In 1988 the Baltimore Orioles Major League Baseball team made history by starting the season with 21 straight losses. It was such a freakish failure it almost took special talent to lose that consistently.

In 2008 and 2009, Americans lost $9.8 trillion in wealth during the Great Recession. The value of our homes plunged, retirement accounts vanished overnight, and global economic growth plummeted. Huge banks closed their gilded doors and others were bailed out by the government. This was the greatest economic disaster since the Great Depression.

In 2002, AOL Time Warner posted the biggest annual corporate loss in history—a staggering $98.7 billion ($140.2 billion in today's money). America Online (AOL) struggled, top executives resigned, and the loss was twice what Wall Street expected. Ouch.

It's easy to see—*and feel*—the loss in each event.

If you ever played sports, losing a game stinks, but going 0–21 is demoralizing. If you lived through the Great Recession, you remember the global gut punch and panic those overnight losses of wealth caused. If you've ever led a business, posting the largest loss of value in history is unfathomable. Maybe AOL should've kept sending those free internet access CDs after all?

FEEDBACK LOOPS

In a sense, these scenarios offer a final scoreboard to judge winners and losers. Scoreboards are feedback loops, revealing exactly where we stand in relationship to success. You probably use them across the spectrum of your life.

School

What's my grade in math? How many credits have I completed toward my undergraduate degree? How many AP classes should I take? How many days of high school can I miss and still graduate? (True story. It was 25, FYI.)

Business

How many cups of coffee did we sell this week? How did the new Star Wars movie do in the box office? How are the profit margins for our subscription dog treat boxes? What's our net promoter score looking like? Is our churn too high?

Politics

Does our party have control of the House and Senate? How many votes did our candidate get? Are the policies

I support being championed? Are people still mocking us on Twitter? (On Twitter, the answer is always yes.)

Finances

How much have my Roth IRAs grown? How much student loan debt do we have? Is our debt-to-income ratio good enough to get pre-qualified for a mortgage? How much is my Pokemon card collection worth? What's my credit score?

Games

How many hit points do I have left? How many levels have I beaten? What's my KDR (kill/death ratio)? What's my fantasy football rank? Who's got the longest road in Settlers of Catan—and more importantly, how can I ruin it?

Ministry

How many people have put their faith in Jesus? How's end-of-year giving shaping up? What's our ratio of new-to-returning visitors? Is it time to start a second service?

Rewards Points

How many more stars until I get a free burrito? How many frequent flyer miles do we have? How many free hotel nights have I racked up?

#WINNING

Scoreboards make it simple to define winning and losing. That also means it's easy to know how we should feel. If the score goes

Our constant access to analytics and instant feedback comes with a problem: there is no ready-made-scoreboard for our lives.

up, we should feel good. If the score goes down, we should feel concerned. And if the game's over and the other team has more points than we do, we should feel like Minnesota Vikings[1] fans.

Here's the problem. Our personal lives aren't like any of those isolated areas. Instead, they're a complex layering of each. Our constant access to analytics and instant feedback comes with a problem: there is no ready-made-scoreboard for our lives. That doesn't stop us from keeping score though, does it? Internally, we tally points, and those points calibrate our emotional states. But, just like a sport with ill-defined or contradictory rules, we find ourselves in a mess when we don't have a clear definition of what winning looks like.

For instance, what's your personal definition of winning, and which of these things puts points on your scoreboard? Is it ...

- *the car parked in your driveway?*
- *the number of square feet in your house?*
- *the school your kids go to?*
- *the college you went to?*
- *how often you fight—or don't fight—with your spouse?*
- *the amount of money you earn?*
- *the amount of money you give?*

---

[1] Full disclosure: The Vikings are really good this season. So the joke's on me. However, give it a couple of years and this'll be hilarious. Boom, roasted.

- *how tidy your house is?*
- *the number of hours you work each week?*
- *the number of subscribers to your blog?*
- *the number of likes your social media posts get?*
- *your kids' grades in school?*
- *your physical weight on the scale?*
- *your bra size?*
- *your IQ?*
- *how many dates you go on?*
- *making your parents proud?*
- *making sure you've become nothing like your parents?*
- *having your political candidate of choice win?*

It's pretty straightforward to know when we're winning in sports, games, business, and finances. The rules are generally clear, and so are the stakes. If we have fewer points than our opponents, we lose. If we have more expenses than income, we lose. If we have zero hit points, we lose. In those areas, "Game Over" is predictable—and we know the stakes.

Winning at life doesn't work like that.

LOCK AND KEY

Imagine you've had a special key for as long as you can remember. Now imagine you're walking through a hallway with nearly endless doors of every shape and size. Some are ancient oak, sturdy and worn. Others are polished french doors with luxurious curtains pulled tight. Others are sleek and modern, plain and boring, round like a Hobbit door.

Over the years, you watch parents, friends, celebrities, teachers, and strangers go in and out of doors. Excited, you follow, trying your key in door after door. Not one of them opens for you. You're frustrated. What good is a key that won't open any doors?

So, you follow other people into their rooms, squeezing in before the door shuts. Some of the rooms are cool. The people are nice and the views inspiring. Others are terrible. The people are rude, the decor is drab, and just being there makes your skin crawl.

None of these rooms leaves you satisfied. A gnawing feeling reminds you to search for the room your key is meant to open.

Back in the eternal hallway, you pull out your key to try one more door. You boldly stride up to a bright yellow one beaming like pure sunshine. You slide your key into the lock, give it a hopeful twist, and... nope. Not this one either. You twist harder and angrily ram your shoulder into the happiest door in the hallway.

Then you hear a voice.

"Are you alright?"

You turn, annoyed. It's an older man with a smile.

"My key doesn't work," you reply shortly.

"Oh, that's odd. What number is on it?"

Your brow furrows. "What number?"

"You know, the little number on your key that tells you which door to unlock."

He holds up his key. It looks different than yours. It's older and larger. And, it has a number.

"Why don't we take a look at your key?" he suggests.

You look again, and there it is, a number you never noticed before. It doesn't match the number on the yellow door. All that pacing, frustration, time and energy spent watching where everyone else was going—all in vain because you didn't match *your* key to *your* door.

No, life isn't always as simple as fitting a key into the right door, but what I'm asking you to do is reflect on your mindset. Look closely at your life goals and ambitions, and check the number on your key. Does it actually match the door you're trying so desperately to get through?

Maybe you know exactly where you're headed. You know your purpose forward and backward, and have a plan. However, I wrote this book on the chance that maybe you're like me. For the longest time, I broke myself against the wrong door. And it wasn't until I took a strategic pause that I realized my definition of winning—*or getting through the right door*—was off base.

WAYPOINTS

In this book, we're working to win—together. But the idea isn't simply to achieve more goals, make more money, lose more

In this book, we're working to win—together. weight, gain more followers, build a bigger business, or any other ideas of success the world has thrown at us. Any of those could be the result (like they were for me), but they won't be our North Star. Instead, our work is about the journey as much as it is the result.

We're going to win at the game that really matters to us. And the system I'll share, called your Life Scoreboard, is based on two conversations I had about ten years apart that changed the trajectory of my life. The first was with a man in my church, and the second was a conversation with my wife (stay tuned). Let's begin with the first.

CHAPTER TWO:

A LESSON IN BURNT PIZZA

Have you ever sat alone in your underwear and felt overwhelmingly inadequate?

I was 21, sitting in my wife's and my first apartment, playing video games in my boxers. It was noon on my day off, so I'd almost grown into the couch at this point. The TV blared with gunfire, adrenaline pumped through my veins, and a frozen pizza sizzled in the oven. In my early twenties, this was the stuff of great days.

(Priorities—I know.)

In my trance-like state I barely heard my phone ring. I didn't know the number, but my Team Deathmatch round of Call of Duty had just ended, so I answered.

"Hello?"

"Hi, Pastor Jordan, do you have a minute to talk?" a man asked.

I didn't immediately recognize his voice, as he sounded like he'd been crying.

"Sure thing. And sorry, may I ask who's calling?" I asked.

"It's Gary," he said.[2] "We've got a big problem on our hands..."

Silence.

I took my dorky headset off, leaving the chatter of other gamers, and leaned forward to concentrate. What he told me next was disturbing, heartbreaking, and miles above my pay grade.

You see, I did a brief stint as an interim preaching pastor at a small church in a small town about an hour away from us. Gary and his wife attended there. To me, this was a dream gig. For most of my life, I believed I was *supposed to be* a full-time pastor. And I was convinced that unless I had this specific job title, there was no way I would be fulfilled, happy, or serving my purpose. So getting the chance to preach every Sunday for six months, even to 50 people or so, was a mountaintop experience.

I grew up a PK (church lingo for Pastor's Kid). In fact, both of my parents are still pastors and have led churches in various capacities for decades. I witnessed their impact firsthand. They raised up leaders, planted churches, and opened our home to broken people

---

[2] Name changed to respect privacy.

who needed to heal. The way they served naturally drew me to the pulpit.

So there I was, in my early twenties, thinking I was stepping into my destiny. But my conversation with Gary shocked me like the Ice Bucket Challenge.

"WHAT DO I DO?"

Gary poured out his painful dilemma.

"We just found out that my son was molesting our daughter for years when they were children. My daughter and wife want me to turn him in to the authorities and cut him off from our family."

My blood ran cold. I started to panic. I was out of my depth.

Gary kept on, "If I don't side with my wife and daughter, I'm afraid I'll lose them forever. But if I cut my son out of our lives, I will lose him forever, and I don't know what will happen to him."

Then, he asked: "Pastor Jordan, what do I do?"

My video game started without me. My character stood lifeless on the screen. The oven beeped. My teammates squalled on the headset, wondering why I'd disengaged. The world kept spinning, but I felt totally paralyzed by the weight of Gary's heartbreak. I prayed. *Holy Spirit, please give me something—anything—that can help.*

I responded slowly, carefully.

"Gary, I'm so sorry this happened. I can't imagine how painful this must be. First of all, I think you, your wife, and your daughter need to see a good Christian counselor. This is too deep to wade through on your own."

I paused for a second, praying again.

"Here's the limited advice I can offer. You're a dad who needs to protect his family. Right now, you learned your daughter was badly hurt. She's still being hurt by this. And so is your wife, and so are you. You need to guard them right now and do what's best for your son. You don't know what else he's done, or what else he'll do."

I could hear Gary continue to cry on the other end.

"I believe the right thing to do is stand by your wife and daughter. And then help your son by bringing this to the right people. If you hide this, you're going to lose your girls and allow your son to be a secret monster. That will eat him alive and may even hurt other people."

I waited, hoping this was helpful.

"Okay, that's what I thought," he said. "Thanks and I'm sure you're very busy, so I appreciate your time. I'll see you on Sunday."

Click.

I smelled burnt pizza. I didn't care. I sat on the couch, stunned. I felt overwhelmed by the high stakes of pastoring. These were people's lives, and they looked to me for help in their deepest pain.

Gary's family went through a string of hard seasons, and I don't know if my counsel was any help. What I do know is there was a lesson I should

These were people's lives, and they looked to me for help in their deepest pain.

have learned immediately—but wouldn't grasp for years.

This was the first conversation, and provides the lesson at the heart of this book. The second conversation was with Joelle, my wife, and it was a doozy, acting as a catalyst for the Life Scoreboard system itself.

WHAT GAME ARE YOU PLAYING?

You've likely had similar moments in your life. Dramatic (or even traumatic) experiences when you stare wide-eyed at the intensities of life. While it took a decade to realize, my conversation with Gary brought something into focus: *I spent my twenties playing the wrong game.*

I believed I was chasing a life of big impact, like my parents lived. I believed there were thousands of souls like Gary who desperately needed wisdom from a brilliant kid like me. And, I believed that until the title of pastor was attached to my name full-time, I wouldn't, and couldn't be fulfilled—because every minute outside professional ministry was 60 seconds of the world missing out on what I had to offer.

I can still hear Gary's voice addressing me as "Pastor Jordan." Today the title rings hollow. And it's not because God didn't want to use me to lead people into his grace and goodness, but because I set my eyes on the wrong person. My gaze wasn't fixed with compassion on Gary, and certainly not on God's glory before my own. My stare was locked on the mirror, seeing myself and my own needs first.

I chased something outside God's purpose for me. I struggled with pride, but most of my issue was insecurity. I had to be a pastor. Otherwise, what was I worth? I had an identity issue.

My game of success had goalposts of full-time ministry, but I spent ten years frustrated and failing to score because I played the wrong game. Ironically, today I'm a teaching pastor, a middle and high school Bible teacher to students in four different countries, and lead a 501(c)(3) called Short Daily Devotions, where we reach tens of thousands with Bible-based devotions in nearly 100 countries.

None of these are full-time—and in fact, I don't take a salary. The funny cherry on top is that I'm not quite God's gift to humanity like I thought I was. I'm just an average dude who talks a lot about the Bible (sometimes aggressively inarticulate, other times moderately helpful).

God was preparing me for my purpose according to His process, not mine. But until I gave up my self-centered motives (which is still a daily necessity), I didn't pursue much outside of soothing my own insecurities.

We each need to know what game we're really playing and whether we want to spend our lives playing it. Is it yours—or the one you think is expected of you? Is it the one a cultural narrative says will make you happy? Is it the one that looks safest because non-failure has become your definition of success?

Here's the danger. When we don't know the *true* game, we don't know the *true* rules. Imagine a football player who runs backward every time he touches the ball because he's confused on which endzone equals a touchdown. No matter how hard he sprints, he's going to spend his career losing. Why? He's running the wrong way. In fact, the harder he runs, the faster he'll lose.

I don't mean that life is a low-stakes game or your purpose is as simple as scoring a few points, but it's been a one-to-one analogy for my life. In my pursuit of becoming a full-time pastor and church planter, I imagined preaching to growing crowds of people, hungry to radically change their lives. That was the endzone. The grand slam. The goal. That's the place my worth was found.

> *When we don't know the* true *game, we don't know the* true *rules.*

Pastoring proved a different picture than I'd painted in my head. The shockwave of responsibility reverberated far beyond a Sunday morning message. I wanted to make a positive impact on people, but I had the path wrong in two key ways:

1. *It was all about me.*
2. *It was all about what I was "supposed" to do.*

DELIGHTING IN THE JORD

My deadliest sin was selfishness. It isn't wrong to desire fulfillment and satisfaction—in fact we should pursue both. King David, the Bible's beloved warrior-poet even penned a Psalm about this, saying the Lord "will give you the desires of your heart." This means what we want most deeply is what God will give to us if we follow him, right?

Actually, no. And therein lies the trouble. Those aren't the "rules" to the game. Did you notice I actually started halfway through that Bible verse? I wrote my own hook. Here is Psalm 37:4 in full:

> *Delight yourself in the Lord,*
> *and he will give you the desires of your heart.*

I tried skipping to the end where I got what I wanted, and then ret-rofitted that wish onto God's will. I missed the part about delighting myself in the Lord.

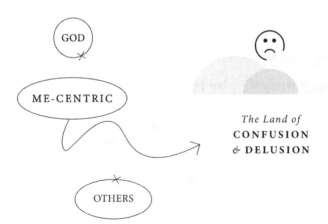

My starting place was "me-centric" rather than "God-centric." My significance and potential were dependant upon a title—on something I could earn. It's funny how beginning with self-as-center actually puts a wet blanket on the blaze of glory our lives can be.

It isn't until we stop and challenge the game we're playing—*the victory we're after*—that we can see whether or not we're pursuing something valuable beyond ourselves. And fundamentally, I believe achieving what matters most will fulfill God's purpose, be for others' good, and result in our personal fulfillment.

Why? Because what we pursue determines who we become. We transform to the magnitude of impact required of us. I spent much of my time living small—playing video games, seeking comfort, living for entertainment, addicted to food, drawn to pornography, and more—because these actions were in line with my pursuit of self-gratification. But it wasn't until I elevated my horizon (delighting in the Lord rather than the Jord!) that I had to become more.

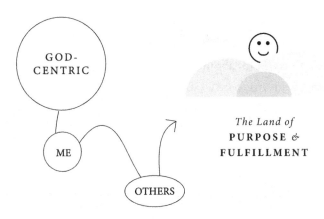

What you pursue determines who you become.

So, my friend, what does winning look like for you? What game are you playing? How do you put points on the scoreboard of purpose? Ultimately, what are you chasing?

What you pursue determines who you become.

MISPLACED HOPE

A number of years ago, I worked with a men's discipleship ministry. We hosted training opportunities, and during one event, I shuttled our keynote speaker around for the weekend. Little did I know that meeting Norm Wakefield, founder of Elijah Ministries, would change my life.

Norm is a slim, white-haired man with a military bearing. His wisdom, Biblical fluency, and character remind me of the giants of the Bible—Moses, Paul, John the Baptist, you get the picture. This guy was on fire and I lit my spiritual candle at his flame. I learned so many things from him about what it means to be a man, and even more, what it means to be a human created in God's image with a purpose.

Norm helped me dethrone myself from the center of my life and look to the One infinitely more worthy (and capable) of that chair… Jesus. Among his pearls of wisdom, Norm said something that deeply impacted my life.

"Whoever has your hope, has your heart," he said, pointedly, during one of his training sessions.

That statement stopped me like a snoot full of buckshot. He explained that when we place our hope for a better future in someone or something, that person or thing automatically owns our heart. They have captured our fundamental desires and daily pursuits. They shape our lives.

Scripture continually talks about the heart as the place of a person's identity. It's our ruling center, seat of willpower, and essence of character. So in a genuine sense, whatever (or whoever) has our *heart* has *us*. And we will chase that person or thing as supreme, above all else. Simply put, achieving it becomes our working definition of winning.

My burning desire for this title of pastor was misplaced hope. I thought if I became a pastor, everything would fall into place. The desires of my heart would be fulfilled, I would be living my purpose, my marriage would instantly be fixed, and my struggles would evaporate. I could finally become who I was meant to be... but *only if* I stepped into my coveted gig.

Actually, God was more interested in me becoming the man I was supposed to become, with the character I was supposed to develop, long before I possessed a title that was too heavy for me to carry. As He loosed these shackles from my heart, He revealed that what I *thought* I wanted, I didn't actually want. And more importantly, I could stop chasing.

GOD-SIZED

I've worked with hundreds of different people in my yarn-ball of a career, and it has been the greatest honor to have collaborated with dozens of authors, ghostwritten more than 30 books, and help publish dozens more.

Helping someone write a book means you connect with them at a deep level. You ask questions nobody asks, dive into their psyche, and crawl into their mind to draw out their most colorful life experiences. The summit for many of these books has been cataloguing a leader's journey, codifying the principles and action plans that have made them so incredible.

As I look at my life reflected in so many of their journeys, I clearly see I suffered from this disease of misapplied hope. One of these leaders, author and coach Doug Wood, helped me discover something profound:

> *No title gives you permission to make the impact you were designed to make. You achieve what matters most to you by aligning your actions with your vision, and your effort with your milestones.*

Now, let me ask you: What do you want?

I'm not asking what your parents, or the church, or the education system wants for you. What do *you* want? If you get radically honest, you'll discover desires placed inside of you so big they actually seem far fetched. They are there for a reason—they are

God-sized. When you discover what God really wants for you, an incredible thing happens, life stops becoming about you.

Counterintuitive, I know.

I have seen this play out dozens of times while working with high-performance people. From multi-millionaires and executive teams of billion-dollar companies, to former CIA agents and nonprofit leaders, the truth comes down to

If you get radically honest, you'll discover desires placed inside of you so big they actually seem far fetched. They are there for a reason—they are God-sized.

this: your greatest impact on the world will come from the way you pour into other peoples' lives. Pursuing a God-sized call can, and will, change the world in wonderful ways.

MULTIPLY

We are blessed to be blessings. We see this throughout Scripture. God blessed Abraham so every nation would be blessed through him (Genesis 22:18). He's prepared good works for us to walk in, bless others, and show Jesus (Ephesians 2:10). He calls his people to be a light of hope and salvation to all nations (Isaiah 49:6). And He creates such a rich life in us that we overflow with blessings to others:

> *"Land that drinks in the rain often falling on it and that produces a crop useful to those for whom it is farmed receives the blessing of God. But land that produces thorns*

*and thistles is worthless and is in danger of being cursed. In
the end it will be burned."* (Hebrews 6:7–8 NIV)

Fundamentally, Christians are producers. We multiply grace even
as we consume it. Here's the deal: *it doesn't go well for the folks
who consume but never bloom.* They're the ones who produce
thorns and thistles, patches of prickly dirt that only suck the life
out of what's around them. They don't produce any fruit beneficial
for others. They are "me-centric" brambles that need to be transformed or torn out. (AKA: me in my twenties.)

> *Here's the deal:
> it doesn't go well
> for the folks who
> consume but
> never bloom.*

Why am I so passionate about all this
"self-improvement" stuff? Because
growth, transformation, and multiplication of our capacity to give life to
others is key to the flourishing of the
nations and our God-honoring personal fulfillment. To me, these pas-
sages (and those like them) form the theological foundation for
discovering our purpose, pursuing growth, and then producing
fruit like mad.

Even better, those loony, far-fetched visions to change the world
we're almost ashamed to speak out loud are simply waiting for two
things. First, for us to take faithful action and sprint toward the
finish line God has set before us (Hebrews 12:1–2). Second, for
Jesus to pick up our meager offering of five loaves and two fish and
multiply it so it can feed the multitudes.

Do you remember that story? Evening falls on the foothills
of Galilee, and though Jesus sought a quiet place (because his

cousin, John the Baptist, had just been murdered), thousands of people followed him for miles. Instead of playing video games in his underwear and growing annoyed when people in his church called, Jesus had "compassion" on every one of them (Matthew 14:14). Compassion means "to suffer with." So, when their hearts hurt, his heart hurt.

Another way to describe this could be, "Today, we hurt." So Jesus spent the rest of the day healing them. And as if that wasn't enough, he fed them. How did he do it? A little boy brought his sack lunch, willing to give everything he had to feed the people who came to see Jesus. Food wasn't the only thing multiplied that day—faith, compassion, and wholeness were as well.

I'm passionate about achieving everything I'm capable of in life because I know that, even though I'm a nothing-burger on my own, Jesus can turn my life into something helpful and nourishing for the world.

SPIRITUAL PROPOSITIONS OF GROWTH

Our mindset on personal growth and achievement must start from a God-centric position, understanding these five propositions:

1. *God created me for a purpose.*
2. *My purpose will be aligned with God's vision to redeem the world.*
3. *Everything I have, and am, is to multiply his goodness for others.*

4. *Growing in mind, body, spirit, and fulfillment is worship.*
5. *I worship God by pursuing his purpose in my life.*

Are you willing to be multiplied? Are you willing to pursue a God-sized purpose? Are you willing to risk being a countercultural weirdo who doesn't chase after the wrong things?

> *Are you willing to risk being a countercultural weirdo who doesn't chase after the wrong things?*

Please understand, writing this book has convicted me. I'm not the golden boy of purposeful living—my nature is selfish, self-conscious, and self-destructive. However, I am serious about a community that wins together, pushes back darkness, and champions light. I have a lot of growth ahead of me to be the kind of massively fruitful land Hebrews 6 showcases. So, I'm going to do everything I can to prepare the soil for multiplication.

I believe you are reading this because you want the same: to leave a legacy of significance and impact. I invite you to decide what you really want your days on this earth to mean. Imagine how your footsteps will echo into eternity. You have one life, and so do I.

Let's let a sense of urgency settle into our bones.

CHAPTER THREE:

IT'S YOUR TIME

Imagine you die.

Let's say you pass on peacefully in your sleep—or while skydiving. I'll let you pick. Either way, you went fast. However, instead of being ushered through the pearly gates, you find yourself in line. Apparently Saint Peter has a backlog of new arrivals and wait times are a killer. You stand on your tiptoes and crane your neck to see just how far this line stretches, but all you see is an endless line of surprised people.

You notice a strange booth to your right. People shuffle up to a window, get their hand rubber-stamped by an angel with a bell hop's cap, and disappear through solid gold french doors.

The sign above the doorway reads: WELCOME TO YOUR FUNERAL (Limited Showtimes Available).

A few newbies materialize behind you, baffled. You're unsure how long you've been waiting, but the line hasn't budged. Curious, you drift over to the procession and step up to the booth window. You stretch out your hand and feel the cool ink kiss your skin. It's a black question mark.

"Excuse me," you say.

The angel smiles. "Yes?"

"What is this?" You point toward the doors.

"It's a movie of your funeral," the angel says.

You freeze.

"Well, more of a livestream, really. Are you going in?" the angel asks.

"Do I want to?" You rub your thumb over the unsettling mark on the back of your hand.

"That depends."

"On what?"

The angel pauses, looking deeply into your eyes, as if he sees directly into your soul.

"It depends on *who* you lived for."

"What do you mean?" you ask.

"The impact of your life is reflected on the faces of everyone who will stand at your graveside today," the angel explains. "Your legacy will be written through the way people think, speak, and live because of their interactions with you."

He reaches out and gently takes your marked hand.

"If you walk through those doors, you will catch a glimpse of how much your life mattered to people beyond yourself. But you'd better hurry, it's about to begin."

You look from the angel to the doors. They swing open, revealing a dark, empty theater with a giant screen. On that screen is your casket. The doors start closing.

"It's now or never," the angel says.

"Thanks," you blurt out before dashing through the doors and slipping into the darkness.

THE DASH

When you read that story, whose faces populate the crowd? Sure, your friends and family, but who else?

I thought intentionally about my own funeral for the first time about five years ago through an exercise called *the dash*. The idea is to think about your tombstone and the dash placed between your birth and death years. For me, it'll probably be something like this:

Jordan Loftis
1987–2067

Depending on what I do with pizza, I'll live longer than that, but whatever dates are on my tombstone, this experiment forced me to ask what my dash will have meant on this earth.

It was a moving, profound experience, but I forgot about it until I found myself in an old lounge that had been converted into a library in the French Quarter of New Orleans, Louisiana.

MY EULOGY

My wife and I traveled to a life planning retreat, where organizers, led by the dynamic leader Phil Nicaud, challenged us to write our own eulogies. I settled at a table with a chess board top, and pushed back the pieces to make room for my notebook and coffee. The chess pieces formed a semi-circle in front of me, almost like a crowd gathered to memorialize my interment.

It's a heavy thing to do. Honestly, it makes you question how to measure a life well-lived. While I wrote the words I *hoped* my eulogy would contain, a thought struck me: *what a tragedy it would be to attend my own funeral only to realize I spent most of my life living for myself.*

YOUR DASH

Of course, you knew this was coming. It's your turn to pen your own eulogy. You can go free-form or answer these questions to spark your thoughts. Pause here and give yourself space for some soul-searching.

- *What does life look like without you?*
- *What do you hope to have accomplished?*
- *Who benefitted from your life? How?*
- *Why is your death a loss for your community?*
- *What legacy did you leave behind?*
- *How did you spend your time so you died without regret?*

Here's a sampling from mine:

Jordan Loftis lived for others, leading them to the greatest, most beautiful gifts in life: the ability to find and fulfill their purpose, inspiration to grow, and a relationship with Jesus Christ.

His wealth was never hoarded, but multiplied and shared. God gave growth and increase because Jordan was faithful in exponentially increasing what was entrusted to him.

He walked both of his daughters down the aisle, giving them away to tremendous men of character, action, and godliness. He guided his son to become the leader, pillar, father, husband, and disciple he is today.

His relationships with his kids are forged of gold because of his gentleness, openness, and love for them. He leaves them with a lifetime of memories from every continent, culture, and adventure this world has to offer.

Even more, he leaves his greatest prize, treasure, and crown, Joelle Danna, with a legacy of a husband who championed her, put her first, made her laugh until her sides hurt, and loved her as well as any man can this side of eternity.

His impact flowed from the fountainhead of Jesus Christ— the only Vine of eternal life. He leaves an inheritance of generational wealth that blesses many, even outside of his family. The Father was pleased with his son, Jordan.

P.S. Brandon, Jordan asked me to specifically mention that Mom said he was the favorite.

Alright, now it's your turn. Take a few minutes to write your own.

MY EULOGY

SEE IT, CHANGE IT

Are your actions aligned with the memories you hope people will have of you? If you desperately hope to be remembered as a "good" husband and father—or wife and mother—what does "good" mean to you? And are you on that path?

Confession time... I'm raising my hand here. I want that. But what does it require? Time, margin to be mentally and emotionally present, and a selfless, consistent pouring into my wife and kids. Relationships don't flourish on their own. Fertile soil doesn't prepare itself. Seeds don't plant themselves. A garden doesn't tend itself. In full transparency, this year, my actions didn't reflect this vision because I worked too much.

> *Are your actions aligned with the memories you hope people will have of you?*

Here's the great news: *I see it, so I can change it.*

What needs to change for you? What ambitions awakened through reflection? I certainly don't envision my tombstone reading: "Here lies Jordan Loftis, video-game-playing, underwear-loving, pizza-eating goober who wasted his life in front of a glowing screen."

Each one of us has the ability to produce incredible fruit, and if you need to course correct, now is the time. The thought of living a life of irrelevance sends shivers down my spine. By "irrelevance" I don't mean my life is worthless. Irrelevant actually means to be disconnected from something. I desperately don't want to be disconnected from my purpose.

I don't think selfishness always happens because we're terrible people, though, but because we're scared people.

The eulogy exercise stoked a fire in me. It gave me clarity. I don't want to waste my life living for myself. Too many times I've chased comfort over character, satisfaction over servanthood, and instant gratification over impact. I don't think selfishness always happens because we're terrible people, though, but because we're scared people.

A FATE WORSE THAN DEATH

Fear. What are we afraid of?

Often, we're scared of what everyone else thinks. It's funny, because for most of us, our junior high jitters of being the friendless kid in the lunch line never really go away.

For proof, consider the number one human fear: public speaking. You've likely heard this statistic before, but researchers have found that people are more scared to talk in front of a group of people than they are to die.[3] That's right, giving a speech is considered a fate worse than death by most adults on this planet. As irrational as that sounds, it's in perfect alignment with a fundamental human truth. We are deeply afraid of being ostracized and rejected.

---

[3] Dwyer, Karen & Davidson, Marlina. (2012). Is Public Speaking Really More Feared Than Death? Communication Research Reports. 29. 99–107.

To achieve what matters most, we must first press the reset button, question the game we're playing, and ask ourselves whose approval we are actually living for: *our own or others*? After my sermonizing on selflessness, it may seem contradictory to ask you to live for your own approval. But here's what I mean for us.

Each night, our heads should hit the pillow completely satisfied with our tenacity in pursuing our purpose. We should end each day with the confidence we pursued our purpose with vigor.

This is the approval we should strive for, one that results in a clear conscience. It is confidence we're putting points on the right scoreboard, and it's fearlessness to risk, jump, and look different.

The trouble is, that white-hot desire might be lost deep within our hearts, like an ancient fire burning in a forgotten mine.

The trouble is, that white-hot desire might be lost deep within our hearts, like an ancient fire burning in a forgotten mine. For some of us, what we *really want* to achieve in the world needs to be excavated. It's buried under years of fear, guilt, or false expectations. Sometimes, it's even obscured by focusing on things with no eternal value.

SQUASH PERFECTIONISM

Imagine your life as currency. Did you know you define your own exchange rate? Where you invest your time defines what you're willing to exchange it for, and you make hundreds of these

ery day. Look at the last week, year, or even decade—
did you assign yourself? Are you pursuing a purpose
re maximally valuable? Or have you been putting it off
for the *right time*?

Perfectionism. Procrastination is delaying what we know
It is a deadly we should be doing. (I'm sure I'm the only
one who's ever done this!) Did you know
disease. that fear of failure drives procrastination?
If you've ever felt that sapping of motivation and empty energy
tank, even when you *know* you've got key actions to take, consider
that fear (or perfectionism) may be driving you.

- *We doubt we'll be able to accomplish something, so we put it off...*
- *We're so scared to fail it paralyzes us...*
- *We only do safe things because they don't threaten our identities...*

What is the root of each of these fears? Perfectionism. It is a deadly
disease. In fact, tragic as it is, researches found perfectionist con-
cerns correlate to suicide ideation.[4] The researchers concluded:

*Results lend credence to theoretical accounts suggesting
self-generated and socially-based pressures to be perfect are*

[4] Smith, Martin M., Simon B. Sherry, Samantha Chen, Donald H. Saklofske, Christopher Mushquash, Gordon L. Flett, and Paul L. Hewitt. "The Pernicious-ness of Perfectionism: A Meta-Analytic Review of the Perfectionism–Suicide Relationship." Wiley Online Library. John Wiley & Sons, Ltd (10.1111), September 4, 2017. https://onlinelibrary.wiley.com/doi/abs/10.1111/jopy.12333.

part of the premorbid personality of people prone to suicide ideation and attempts. Perfectionistic strivings' association with suicide ideation also draws into question the notion that such strivings are healthy, adaptive, or advisable.

Before we go any further, I want to release you from any unhealthy standards of perfection. Be released from any guilt in failing in certain areas of your life. And more, as Christians, remember where condemnation originates: *Satan.* The

The Holy Spirit convicts and draws; the Accuser condemns and separates.

Holy Spirit convicts and draws; the Accuser condemns and separates. Instead of staying stuck, I want to invite you to embark on a new journey today with fresh hope. Believe, deep down that it's your time to win, and achieve what matters most to you.

IT'S YOUR TIME

One year ago, Joelle and I stood on the cusp of kicking off our new marketing and publishing company with hesitation, much like fuzzy baby birds about to leap out of the nest, hoping to fly before the great splat.

To mix analogies, we planned to build the plane as we flew it. It was scary, but not trying was scarier. And since then, this phrase has come to represent what we're about: *it's your time.* So much so, it's what we named our second business, It's Your Time Wellness.

It's a mindset you can own, as well.

First of all, it means it's your season. The time has finally come for you to win in the ways you have never won before. It means positioning yourself to win battles you've repeatedly lost. How long have you listened to fear and failure whisper, "You'll never beat this... Never achieve this... Never amount to your silly dreams..." It's your time, even if you've never had the support system or mindset to get there.

Secondly, it means it's your life. It is not anyone else's, it is yours. You have 1,440 minutes every single day, just like the rest of us. You have power over, control of, and responsibility for how you spend those precious minutes.

Not your job—you.

Not your family—you.

Not your parents—you.

Not your friends—you.

Not your limitations—but your expectations.

You have a responsibility to multiply what you have been given.

GROWTH OR DIE

There's a famous parable, called the Parable of the Talents, in Matthew Chapter 25. Jesus shared this story more than 2,000 years ago and it's still changing the world today.

Three guys worked for the same boss. Before going on a trip, the boss gave each man money. He handed the first worker five talents, the second three talents, and the third one talent. While away, he expected his guys to put the money to work, multiplying it. Here's what they did.

The man with five talents made some clever trades, doubling his master's investment. The man with two talents followed suit, and doubled his talents, as well. But the guy with one talent dug a hole and buried it, scared his boss would be angry if he lost the money. If he couldn't be perfect, he wasn't going to try. A fear of failure kept him hiding in a hole rather than fighting in the arena.

While the story has a few applications, they share the same core principle: we are made to multiply the investments entrusted to us. This means multiplying our faith, our natural skills and abilities, our money, and our resources.

We are entrusted with "gold" to multiply its value by sharing with others. Sometimes we mess that up. We either hoard what we've been given, keeping it to ourselves. Or, we hide what we've been given, so we don't lose it.

Jesus says both of those options are wrong. Instead, we're mandated to multiply our talents. When we look at Jesus' life, he literally did this with his own body. He lived as the only perfect person ever on this planet, then paid the price for us by dying on the cross. And what did this great risk and sacrifice do? It multiplied God's grace for the entire world. Honestly, it shows us that many times the "safe" choice is actually the "sinful" choice.

Growth and multiplication come from risk, discomfort, and a willingness to die to ourselves rather than hoarding or hiding. In the end, even the very things people hoard and hide will be taken from them and proverbially given to those who will follow the mandate to multiply the good things given to them.

The stakes are clear: growth or die. It's actually a pretty shocking parable. The stakes are clear: growth or die. As Jesus said, "To everyone who has will more be given, and he will have an abundance. But from the one who has not, even what he has will be taken away. And cast the worthless servant into the outer darkness. In that place there will be weeping and gnashing of teeth" (Matthew 25:28–30 ESV).

Yowza.

Notice it wasn't about the number of talents, but the quality of risk-taking action with an aim to multiply. It's not our wealth or natural abilities that define how successful we are, but whether or not we're doing something with them. Fear is the force that keeps us playing small. It's the force that tries to find any and every reason for not pushing, growing, and multiplying.

It's also at war with stewardship.

STEWARDSHIP

In the Middle Ages, stewardship was a job description. A steward managed large households, properties, finances, and other holdings entrusted to them. But this person was in charge of more than counting beans and rolling rocks in the right direction. A steward was careful and responsible for the growth and well-being of an entire enterprise. As time wore on, the term upgraded, describing leaders of law courts, unions, and other organizations.

From the outset, God commissioned humans as stewards of creation. He blessed us *and* gave us responsibility over everything He made. Our fundamental role is to be "fruitful and multiply" (Genesis 1:28), exercising responsible authority. This glorifies God and blesses all creation. Regardless of our spiritual affiliations (or non-affiliations), I believe people were blessed to be blessings on this earth. We bear responsibility for how we prosper the time, talent, and treasure entrusted to us.

We bear responsibility for how we prosper the time, talent, and treasure entrusted to us.

Remember, though, stewardship does not equal perfection. It equals intention. It is consistent, thoughtful, and selfless effort in the right direction.

For the rest of this book, we're going to turn this message into an actionable system called the Life Scoreboard. It's a dashboard to gauge how you're doing in the areas of life that matter most to you—and therefore, the areas you can multiply to benefit those around you. There are five components we'll walk through together:

1. *Choosing a Life Area*
2. *Envisioning your Promised Land*

3. *Setting SMRTY goals to get you there*
4. *Defining your Point-Scoring Actions*
5. *Keeping Score as you multiply the life you've been given*

Understand this: everything starts with a decision to own the way you spend your life. Don't let that scare you away. It's exciting. It's taking to heart God's mandate that we steward well. See this as an invitation to map out your course to fulfill your purpose. So, let's get started.

PART TWO:
YOUR LIFE SCOREBOARD

A system of choosing where to grow,
understanding what growth looks like,
defining how to get there, and knowing
how to win every day.

• • •

*"Where there is no prophetic vision
the people cast off restraint, but blessed
is he who keeps the law."*
Proverbs 29:18

CHAPTER FOUR:

YOUR LIFE SCOREBOARD

In 2011, Republican presidential candidate Rick Santorum listened as Newt Gingrich addressed a crowd on the campaign trail. Or, he pretended to listen, at least. Santorum secretly watched college football on his tablet. That's right, even hopeful presidents keep tabs on scoreboards.

Santorum isn't alone in his obsession, though. A century ago, sports fans fixated on the scores of their favorite teams in much the same way. In 1912, thousands flooded the streets of Washington to witness the World Series results in real time.

Image: The Atlantic

And what was this sea of baseball fans looking at? It wasn't the game itself, and certainly not a live broadcast, or even a recording. It was a scoreboard, updated one play at a time.

Image: The Atlantic

About a decade later, people started purchasing movie tickets to watch the Coleman Life-Like Scoreboard.

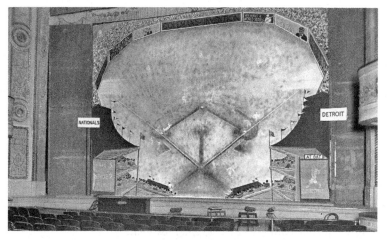

Image: The Atlantic

The "screen" was actually a giant piece of stretched fabric, behind which a group of men used flashing lights to show the action of the game.

Image: The Atlantic

It's a fact, we love scoreboards. We're obsessed with knowing who won, and scoreboards are our cultural method of choice. Here's how Joelle and I built them for our lives. If you're like us, endlessly busy and running without an end in sight, you'll be able to relate—and the system will mean that much more to you.

THE SCOREBOARD CONVERSATION

The last year has been a wickedly exciting blur. But the funny thing about excitement is that it brings a lot of discomfort. One of my favorite writers, G.K. Chesterton, said, "An adventure is simply an inconvenience rightly considered." If that's the case, we've been regular Indiana Joneses during the past year.

Twenty nineteen has been a time of great change and upheaval in our lives, and it all started at Panera Bread on the day after Thanksgiving in 2018 in Rapid City, South Dakota. Heavy, wet snowflakes swirled like stars falling from the sky, the kind you could almost hear when they hit the earth.

It was the first outing my wife and I had been on without our 6-month-old twins and three-year-old daughter in months. We loved them to pieces, but man alive, there are only so many diapers and bedtime shenanigans a person can handle. There were nights when our babies woke up more than ten times. Added to the typical new-parent exhaustion of twins and a toddler was the fact that our babies, Kindy and Wilder, were born prematurely and spent time in the neonatal intensive care unit (NICU).

Wilder spent two months there, and Kindy, one month. Our biggest battle with Kindy was her nasty habit of turning blue. She would stop breathing, which is terrifying. And for those of you not familiar with babies, blue is not a good look for infants.

On top of that, our son had a disease called congenital CMV (cytomegalovirus), a virus that is only a problem when contracted in the womb. It attacks the baby's nervous system and can cause deafness, blindness, and cognitive disabilities, among a host of other things. (It also sounds like a kind of death-dealing dinosaur, which is discomforting.) To treat him, doctors pumped him full of the same antiviral medication used to treat HIV patients.

We floated through life in a sleepless haze, scared and stressed. Now we sat in a booth, in solitude, our babies in the capable hands of my parents. We could breathe for the first time in months.

I needed to tell my wife something and I faced her with butterflies in my stomach.

It was a moment of rest—and a fork in the road. I needed to tell my wife something and I faced her with butterflies in my stomach. I had sworn I would never start another business because the first business I cofounded went... poorly. Yet, here I was, about to pitch another venture. We were still licking our wounds from the last failed business, which was honestly a difficult and humiliating experience for me.

I wasn't excited to dive back into the deep end of a swimming pool I was convinced was still infested with sharks, but I had grown weary with our current arrangement. For five years, I had been working a day job while side-hustling to make ends meet. But now, I had clients pounding at my door with such consistency, there was no way I could serve them and stay at my day job. So we had a choice: stay and settle or swim with the sharks.

We had barely recovered from my previous crash and burn. I had made a serious rookie mistake, failing to diversify our client base. Our biggest client was worth roughly 80 percent of our revenue and when they had a bad quarter, it took us under too. I learned a costly lesson in diversification.

One of my mentors, a brilliant entrepreneur named Rohn Gibson, gave me wisdom during this season I'll never forget.

He asked, "Jordan, why is it safer to stay at your day job?"

The answer was simple.

"Because I have a steady paycheck and health insurance," I said. "Think about my twins and how often they have to be at the doctor."

"So," he prodded me. "There are no insurance options outside of working in your current position?"

"No…" I trailed off. "There are other options."

"So, if you can find a viable insurance option, then what's holding you back?"

I told him it was more than that. What if the work dries up again, like it did last time? He wasn't having it.

"Explain to me how counting on your day job is different than that," he said. "You realize, they could fold or fire you at any time, right?"

I thought in silence. He had made his point. Staying put was nothing more than a false sense of security. Deep down, I just didn't want to fail again.

JUMP

Joelle and I sipped hot coffee as I recounted my conversation with Rohn. Tired and wired at the same time, we weighed the costs. If we wanted life to be different, we actually had to act different. So we spotted the landing and jumped, together.

Right now, I write these reflections in a yurt nestled among cottonwoods lining the Missouri River, exactly one year ago to the week we sat huddled in that booth. We knew God had something big planned, and it was an eerie cocktail of freedom and fear. Even as I sent out invoices, and cashed real checks with enough zeros to support us, I battled anxiety, fear and doubt.

At that point, winning simply meant keeping our new business alive. However, that fear drove me to put in 100-plus hour weeks. I didn't sleep well, I didn't eat well, and I gained 20 pounds in just a few months. And it wasn't muscle. The stress grew so intense I even blacked out one day and collapsed, smashing my face into our floor. I visited the doctor, they ran some tests, and told me I needed to chill out. This was not a banner moment.

FINDING TRUE NORTH

I immediately ignored their advice and sprinted back to my basement office to meet deadlines. Here's the thing, fear can be good, when you're around things like a bear. Fear is a wonderful motivator to run to safety. However, it is not a good North Star to navigate your life.

It drove me to grind my mental and physical health into the ground, leaving my wife dealing with three children (mostly on her own). My in-laws saved our bacon time and time again, helping with the kids, taking care of snow removal and yard work, and doing all the life things I neglected. Joelle felt alone, stranded on an island. All I could think about was growing our business as fast as possible so I didn't fail again.

Now, I can tell you story after story about poor decisions I've made this year that cost us sleep, sanity, and even tens of thousands of dollars. Yep, you read that right. But what I really want to tell you is about the conversation that changed everything. It happened on the heels of an insane summer, and you guessed it, started with me apologizing to my wife for working too much.

UNTO US, A SCOREBOARD IS BORN

It was another exhausting day with semi-cranky children, and amidst the hubbub, I promised Joelle next month would be better. I would travel less and be more present. It hurts to think about it, but I was making promises we both knew wouldn't happen.

On the verge of tears, she threw her hands up in the air.

"I never feel like I'm winning," she said. "Every day, I feel like I'm losing, taking step after step backward."

"I never feel like I'm winning," she said. "Every day, I feel like I'm losing, taking step after step backward."

It finally clicked with me. I had no clue what winning actually looked like to her. I was so hyper-focused on growing our business, making money, and doing big things I never asked what she wanted. Few things are as demoralizing as feeling like you're losing ground in life.

Thankfully, in that moment, the Life Scoreboard was born. I looked at her and really *saw her* for the first time in a long time. I asked, "What does winning look like to you?"

I was really asking her to show me her scoreboard, to help me understand the way she measured her life. Just like all those rabid baseball fans crowding around a board full of names and numbers, I pressed in to see what game she was trying to win.

ACHIEVING WHAT MATTERS MOST

A Life Scoreboard is the way your output is internally tallied, so you feel like you are putting points on the board in the areas that matter most to you. It means you are moving forward.

That day, Joelle and I finally sat down to get it all on paper. It was time to define what winning looked like for each of us.

I sketched some boxes in a journal as we talked, and a scoreboard materialized.

Here, I saw something profound. There were areas of overlap where we were both trying to win. Scoring points looked the same. However, there were also areas where she sought growth, but I was doing nothing to help her. We were on the field together wearing the same jerseys, but I was an unsupportive teammate.

Joelle felt the weight of responsibility for multiplying her life, for bearing fruit that would help others. She was passionate about being a producer. Now, I saw how I could support her.

Since we discovered the scoreboard idea, our marriage, business, and ability to win has improved tenfold. It helped us come into alignment on what mattered most to us. It's still a dance and we're far from perfect, but perfection isn't the goal. Putting points on the board every day is the goal.

Through honest conversation, and the scoreboard, it became clear what living a life of significance looked like for Joelle, and the kind of impact she wanted to leave. As crazy as it seems, this is also why we started our wellness coaching company together. Something helpful was blossoming out of our pain.

Already we've made profound strides in our wellness journeys— physically, mentally, emotionally, spiritually, and more. We also now walk alongside clients as they pursue health in those same ways. I can say, after 11 years of marriage, witnessing my wife utilize her passion and deep generosity to give the gift of health is one of my greatest joys. She reclaimed the best parts of herself and fired back up the cylinders motherhood can so often shut down.

I've never been more inspired by her.

This system opened our eyes to what we can accomplish when we work together, instead of apart. Rather than playing on opposite teams, fighting for resources, time, and attention, we started building a life that fed both our desires. It has grown into something beautiful and we are just getting started.

In the next section, we'll walk through how to build your Life Scoreboard. It doesn't matter if you're married or single, if you own a business or work at a company, lead a ministry or attend college—all that matters is deciding where you want to go *and* grow.

This system, as simple as it is, can make all the difference in helping you achieve what matters most. It's done that for us, and even for a few of our friends we've shared it with.

So now I share it with you.

> *This system opened our eyes to what we can accomplish when we work together, instead of apart.*

THE ANATOMY OF YOUR LIFE SCOREBOARD

Here's what we'll build. Your Life Scoreboard has five components.

1. **Life Area:** Which area of your life do you want to grow exponentially?

2. **Promised Land:** What does winning look like in this area?
3. **Goals:** What goals, or milestones, will take you there?
4. **Point-Scoring Actions:** What are the actions you need to take to put points on the board?
5. **Score:** 100 points means victory—yes, we're going to win.

That's it. Super simple, but effective. Follow the exercises for each component, and take advantage of your free digital workbook you can download, here: https://rebrand.ly/life-scoreboard-workbook

CHAPTER FIVE:

CONQUERING THE WOLF PACK

If you could exponentially improve one area in your life in the next 90 days (or less), what would it be? Would you get to your healthy weight? Develop a non-negotiable devotional habit? Strengthen your marriage? Achieve financial breakthrough? Find a serious relationship? Get off of a certain medication? Land a promotion at your job? Start a business?

Each of those ideas revolve around our health, spiritual life, relationships, and money. While there are endless places to focus your effort, in this chapter, we're going to brainstorm and prioritize one area to pursue dramatic growth.

I've found this process often involves tracing your sources of frequent pain. We'll use two concepts, bright spots and dark spots, to find your focal point. Here's how I found mine.

MEET ME AT THE FLAGPOLE

In the fourth grade, I fell in love with Pringles and video games. It was a match made in heaven for my little brain. However, it was a match made in hell for my burgeoning body and sinking confidence. This was especially evident with girls and swimming pools.

In fourth grade, though, something magical happened. One of the prettiest girls in my class handed me a note written in gel pen and covered with enough perfume to give me a contact high. I was stunned. Kids like me didn't get notes from girls like her.

She must have me confused with someone else, I thought. I hesitantly opened the note that had been carefully folded in an elaborate origami pattern of undying love. It read:

You're hotttttt!!!!! Will you be my boyfriend?
Y or N
Meet me at the flagpole tomorrow morning.
Love,
[Redacted]

I floated home. Lighter and a foot taller, I perched on the edge of my bed, reading and rereading it until suppertime. It was a big deal.

In fact, it was such a big deal, I made sure my mom "accidentally" saw it by leaving it out on my desk. In deep insecurity, I wanted her to know I was really going to be somebody at school, and a girlfriend proved that. (Macho, I know.)

The next morning, I ran to school as fast as my chubby little feet could carry me and arrived at the flagpole before the bell rang. My new girlfriend wasn't there, but I held the application tightly in hand. "Yes" had been checkmarked. It should have been a red flag that only her best friend was there but I forged on, excited and hopeful. She was probably running late beautifying herself to meet me.

"Where is my girlfriend?" I asked innocently.

Her friend struggled to look me in the eye, fidgeting nervously.

"She's not your girlfriend anymore," she said. "She just wanted to know what it would feel like to dump somebody."

My heart sank, and I fought back tears. Instant humiliation.

That insecure voice in my head started telling a story. *How stupid are you to think that a boy like you would end up with a girl like her?* And just like that, my identity as less than desirable and an object of mockery, was instilled. This would be reinforced for the next year. I now had a giant target on my back, and was picked on like nobody's business.

PEACHY

Soon after, my parents bought me a brand new coat, which was wonderful because we live in North Dakota, and winters can get brutally cold. It was a top-of-the-line Columbia, and I was grateful despite one fatal flaw. It was lined with goose down and added about 12 inches to my already robust frame.

Even in the dead of winter, we still played football during recess (tackle when the teachers weren't looking). We formed steady teams. I was the quarterback of the underdogs and outcasts. And the cool kids, also known as the "Wolf Pack" made up the opposing team.

A gaggle of girls sat on the sidelines, cheerleading for the Wolf Pack. We had no cheerleaders, but we played our hearts out. It was also while on the gridiron it became clear my body doesn't sweat like normal humans. Instead, my face turns beet red and emanates enough heat to melt plastic. It's a great genetic feature.

I'm sure you can see it—me running around in my marshmallow coat with a fiery-red face, rolling around in the snow while taking my athletic performance very seriously. Suddenly, one of the kids in the Wolf Pack pointed at me and announced, "Hey, he looks like a peach!"

As if rehearsed, the other kids started chanting in unison, "Peach! Peach! Peach!" I kid you not. It was a scene straight from a movie.

I tried to escape to a nearby swing, but one of the Pack trotted to my side, informing me that the girl I had a secret crush on was reading a love note I had "written" her. The truth is, I did like her, but I hadn't written anyone a love note.

THE NOTE

Like a moth to the flame, I walked toward a semi-circle of smirking classmates who'd formed around her. To my horror, she read the forged letter out loud. It included heartfelt sentiments of my undying love for her, as well as dreams of the most explicit activities fourth grade boys could cook up.

They cackled. The Wolf Pack closed in around me. My fight or flight response kicked in, then quickly gave way to a third option: ugly crying.

Like a moth to the flame, I walked toward a semi-circle of smirking classmates who'd formed around her.

This led directly to awesome-genetic-feature number two: my extremely sensitive gag reflex. As I cried in the cold, my nose filled with snot and I couldn't catch my breath. So I gagged and projected a hearty stream of steaming nacho boat into the air.

The Wolf Pack encircled me, baring their fangs as they laughed at my misfortune, pointing at the injured prey they'd separated from the herd. I'm sure you have plenty of stories of your own when you threw up nacho boat on all the popular kids' snow boots, right? Right.

FIND THE PAIN

Kids are jerks. That's that. We've all dealt with our own Wolf Pack. In the end, it's not about what they do, but how we respond and grow. They hit me at my weak point—being overweight and oversensitive to people's opinions of me. It took me years to realize that I had to take ownership of my insecurities and do something about them.

Thankfully, I lucked into a little growth spurt in high school and into college. But as I got into my twenties, I packed on about

40 pounds too many. And the shame of that little boy standing at the flagpole, of Peach rejected in the den of wolves, clung to me like an emotional puffy coat. Oddly enough, it also plunged me into a decade-long cycle of returning to food as the best manager of my emotions.

Areas of pain like this are often places where we desperately want to win. In this chapter, we're going to take the first step in the Life Scoreboard by defining one key Life Area to find victory in during the next 90 days. While the timeline is up to you, I recommend a tight timeline of 90 days or less so you can gain momentum.

Our purpose now is to identify areas that will exponentially impact your ability to win. This exercise will help shed light on what matters most to you right now, and kick off a plan to fulfilling growth.

FIND YOUR BRIGHT SPOTS

To find the Life Area you want to prioritize growing in, we start with four reflections.

1. *Tell me about a time in your life you feel like you won.*
2. *Tell me about a time in your life you feel like you lost.*
3. *Tell me what winning looks like.*
4. *Tell me what Life Area would make the most positive impact if you could flourish there.*

Start with a time where you feel like you won. It could be a moment like getting recognized for a promotion, or a childhood memory of fishing on a lake with your grandpa. For me, I think back to when Joelle and I lived in St. Paul, Minnesota nearly ten years ago. I struggled with my weight, but made strides toward not just winning the battle of the waistline, but actually training for the Twin Cities Marathon.

I ran along the Mississippi River during the summer. On one of my long days, I ran more than 13 miles across sandy trails and riverbanks. My endorphins kicked in, I hit a good flow and found that runner's high. I felt incredible because I felt like I was winning.

Now, let's focus on your wins. In Chip Heath and Dan Heath's brilliant book *Switch: How to Change Things When Change is Hard*, the authors share a helpful concept called bright spots. Instead of simply focusing on the negative areas that need change, they coach people to focus on the bright spots, or what has gone right for us.

Instead of simply focusing on the negative areas that need change, they coach people to focus on the bright spots, or what has gone right for us.

I want you to write out as many bright spots as you can. It might be something in your health. It might be a relationship, a promotion at work, a financial win. It might be a time where you served someone and it impacted their lives. Whatever it is, I want you to find at least five.

Now, you'll use a tool called the "Five Whys" to analyze these bright spots. I learned this in marriage counseling. Our counselor taught us to ask "why" five times after answering an important question. For instance, if I felt like I won on that 13-mile run in St. Paul, then I would ask why.

1. *Why? Because I felt strong and capable...*
2. *Why? Because I conquered something holding me back...*
3. *Why? Because I was starting to prove I could defeat the parts of myself that I didn't like...*
4. *Why? Because I experienced incredible growth in one of the toughest areas for me to master, which meant I could do it anywhere else. I had struggled to finish things over the long term. However, I stuck with this for more than a month and could already run more than half the distance...*
5. *Why? Because this gave me confidence in every area of my life. I came out on the other side a stronger, more capable, more valuable man...*

This digging could go on forever. It's valuable to go at least five levels deep because it forces us to pry into the real motivations behind our actions. Please take the time to dig deeper into at least one bright spot. Devote some brain cells to it, because it will set you up to cut to the heart of what really matters.

TELL ME ABOUT A TIME IN YOUR LIFE YOU FELT
LIKE YOU WERE WINNING?

WHY?

WHY?

WHY?

WHY?

WHY?

DARK SPOTS

For the next question, tell me about a time in your life when you lost. We will call these your dark spots. These are the black holes of confidence, the evidence for the inner stories we tell ourselves that we will never be enough. We are not strong enough. We are too weak, our character is unrefined, or it's always someone else's fault.

Becoming the Peach on the playground is a dark spot for me. Another is when my company failed and I took a position working for half the salary my family needed. Another dark time was in the hospital, with our oldest daughter almost passing away. Pain carves deep ruts, which makes the dark times in our lives easy to identify.

Now, move into the Five Whys exercise, just like you did with your chosen bright spot. Only this time, pick the dark spot where you feel the deepest sense of pain or losing.

TELL ME ABOUT A TIME IN YOUR LIFE YOU FELT
LIKE YOU WERE LOSING?

WHY?

WHY?

WHY?

WHY?

WHY?

LIFE AREAS BRAINSTORM

Ideally, you will discover a thematic link between one of your bright spots and one of your dark spots. Chubby-little-boy Jordan and marathon-training Jordan remain connected, and because of this, my physical health became the first Life Area I focused on for a 90-day intensive.

While you can choose any area in your life, focus on where you've been stuck. Hone in on the area that has stagnated growth, but has the potential to impact many other areas if positively transformed. Use the mind-map below to brainstorm. You don't have to fill in every circle—though you might.

After you've populated your circles with potential Life Areas, choose three to five, and list them in order of importance. While we'll concentrate on the top spot, it's helpful to have a roadmap of where to go next. Once you get into a rhythm, you can tackle a few areas at once. Massive growth in one area often powers growth in others.

PRIORITIZE 3–5 LIFE AREAS FOR THE NEXT 90 DAYS

#1. _____

#2. _____

#3. _____

#4. _____

#5. _____

YOUR NORTH STAR

If you link where you won, and where you lost, you've located a powerhouse of a North Star. This is the area to radically improve in the next 90 days (or whatever timeline you prefer). While it can be set out for a longer timeline, I want you to think in a smaller time-box so that you can see how quickly you can make great strides.

One of the lies we tell ourselves is that everything has to take years, and even decades. In actuality, switching our mindset can change our lives faster than we ever thought possible. So take the time now to find your area, and then move on to the next step in building your Life Scoreboard.

CHAPTER SIX:

THE PROMISED LAND

Growing up, my Dad took me backpacking in the Bighorn Mountains in Wyoming, forming my great love for adventure and the wilderness. Just a mile into this rugged terrain and you knew you had crossed over from the domain of man to the domain of nature.

Those long treks with my father remind me of the difficult, beautiful terrain of life. You trek through canyons that soar hundreds of feet high, you're dwarfed by towering peaks, and you know there may be fanged predators lurking in the shadows. You climb and sweat and still there are mountains upon mountains to climb, enough that no man could ever summit them all in a lifetime. It's a fresh perspective—this world is big and you are small. And yet, you are here, conquering a part of it and yourself.

It's humbling.

One of my favorite challenges was also one of the simplest, crossing the streams. The wilderness offers no bridges, so, you find your own.

Sometimes it's a log big enough to balance your way across. Other times it's simply stomping through the water, which is my least favorite because wet socks are the Devil's soggy underpants.

The best was the third option—carefully rock-hopping your way to the other side. Now, my Dad, being an athletic guy, could hop rock to rock with the grace of a gazelle. I remember as a kid, even with a 60-pound backpack, he seemed to float across the stones. For me, especially in my porky days, this was a more difficult task.

I studied the rocks, and the gaps between them. Slippery, slimy moss coated some of the stones, so I hunted for the stable, dry rocks that would get me from one side of the riverbank to the other safely (and dry).

This analogy builds the next two sections of your Life Scoreboard. We'll start by finding your Promised Land, or the picture of what winning *looks and feels* like. Then, we'll reverse-engineer your path to getting there.

HOW TO FIND YOUR PROMISED LAND

In the Old Testament, Joshua led the Israelites through the final stretches of desert in an act of obedience to take possession of the Promised Land. Your Promised Land is success in your Life Area. It is achieving the goals necessary to take victory there, and the fruit of achieving it will feed others in surprising ways.

Since my wife and I made the decision to win in our physical health, our family and friends have joined us, as well. Combined, we've lost hundreds of pounds of fat together, and more importantly, radically rewired our minds in the process. Our victory has become a catalyst for others, just like others inspired us.

Your success will do the same.

The endgame of winning isn't about us, it's about what we produce for others. It's about pushing that first domino and sending the rest falling down. As Dave Ramsey is famous for saying, when we harness a "gazelle-like focus" we can win in seemingly impossible ways. Your focus will inspire your sphere of influence—no matter how large—to level up.

Your focus will inspire your sphere of influence— no matter how large—to level up.

How? Remember, the Promised Land in the Old Testament was a land of abundance, a land filled with milk and honey and fruit the size of people's heads. Yes, giants roamed the countryside, but God forged a path to possess the land and live there forever. The Israelites simply had to walk it out. (But remember, simple doesn't necessarily mean easy.) Some rebelled against this journey (Numbers 14). People resist change; let's embrace it.

I walk my publishing clients through an exercise that helps them identify the Promised Land they're trying to guide their readers to, and I like to think of it as a before-and-after picture. Before is the side of the river bank you're on now. After is the other side—a land flowing with milk and honey.

On your current side of the stream you'll define your problems, negative feelings, insecurities, and daily obstacles. Ultimately, it will make you think about your own identity.

Then, you will look hard at the Promised Land on the other side, describing the solutions to your problems and your fresh feelings of winning. What does an average day look like now that you have experienced transformation? And most of all, what is your *true* identity?

Build a better version of yourself, here, and start by outlining the transformation journey in the Life Area you picked last chapter. Answer the following four questions in the "TODAY" column. These answers describe your current reality. Then, answer them again, only projecting yourself into the "FUTURE," when you have achieved significant growth.

I'll give you an example of what it looked like for me in both columns. Then, you can fill in your own Promised Land. In your chosen Life Area, answer these questions for TODAY first:

1. *What problems do you have?*
2. *What negative emotions do you feel?*

3. *What does your average day look like?*
4. *What do your struggles here tell you about your identity?*

Then, let's imagine a bright FUTURE, when you're winning every day in this Life Area:

1. *What does life look like now that you've conquered those problems?*
2. *What positive emotions do you feel?*
3. *What does your new average day look like?*
4. *How would you describe your identity?*

YOUR PROMISED LAND

	TODAY	FUTURE
HAVE	· Food controls me · I use food to self-medicate emotions · I eat when I'm sad, happy, mad, or even scared/anxious · I'm overweight and feel out of control	· I control everything that goes into my body no matter where I am · I deal with anxiety/stress through breathing, talking, and exercise · I am in command of myself and feel AMAZING that I'm dominating here!
FEEL	· I feel weak and hopeless I can change · I'm embarrassed by my appearance · I feel guilty for modeling poor health habits to my kids · I lack the confidence I should have	· I feel confident and strong · I am PASSIONATE about helping my people get out of this cycle · I'm proud my twins will never know a FAT DAD who modeled poor health · I like the way I look and will improve
AVG. DAY	· I eat way too much, way too often · I sneak bites of food when people aren't looking · I sit ALL DAY LONG working · I try new diets every month, but they never work...	· I understand how much food I need · I can wear ANY article of clothing in my closet — nothing's too tight! · Dieting isn't in my vocabulary · I know exactly what to do with food & how to KEEP GROWING my health
IDENTITY	· Even though I know it's a lie, I feel like a weak, selfish husband, dad, and leader · I'm the guy who's willing to leave results on the table because I lack self-control in MANY areas	· This breakthrough has released me from so much self-focus. I KNOW I will make even more impact and help others find & achieve their purpose because I'm not worried about what anyone thinks — just my key peeps

Now, we'll stitch together the answers to our FUTURE state into a PROMISED LAND STATEMENT you'll add to your Life Scoreboard. Here's what my first statement looked like.

> ### PROMISED LAND STATEMENT
>
> TODAY, I <u>control food, it doesn't control me. I'm fit, bold, and ready to serve others...</u>
>
> I FEEL <u>confident, strong, and passionate about inspiring others to get healthy</u>
>
> MY AVG. DAY <u>starts with wearing whatever I want and confidently growing my health</u>
>
> AND I'M THE KIND OF PERSON WHO <u>isn't consumed with what others think of me</u>

Notice, it's not about crafting a well-written, profound piece of literature. It just needs to be honest, simple, and enough to get started. That's all we need, here.

YOUR TURN

Now, it's your turn! Answer the questions for TODAY while envisioning your bright FUTURE. Then craft your own PROMISED LAND STATEMENT.

In the **TODAY** column, answer:

1. *What problems do you have?*
2. *What negative emotions do you feel?*
3. *What does your average day look like?*
4. *What do your struggles here tell you about your identity?*

In your bright **FUTURE** column, answer:

1. *What does life look like now that you've conquered those problems?*
2. *What positive emotions do you feel?*
3. *What does your new average day look like?*
4. *How would you describe your identity?*

YOUR PROMISED LAND	
TODAY	FUTURE

	TODAY	FUTURE
HAVE		
FEEL		
AVG. DAY		
IDENTITY		

Now write a PROMISED LAND STATEMENT based on your bring FUTURE:

PROMISED LAND STATEMENT

TODAY, I _____

I FEEL _____

MY AVG. DAY _____

AND I'M THE KIND OF PERSON WHO _____

This is a powerful exercise, and it's exciting to see such a fresh vision for an exciting future. However, crossing the river can be hard. It's dangerous. The water levels might rise unexpectedly. A rock that looked stable might actually wobble. We're going to make a plan for you to get to the Promised Land, but first we need to remind ourselves of WHY we want to get there in the first place.

Why is it worth pressing through, even when things get hard? It was actually during the hardest parts of my health journey that I discovered my WHY.

FIND YOUR FIRE

Flash back to the life planning retreat in the French Quarter where I wrote my eulogy. Joelle and I had arrived early, and the morning before it started, we walked the streets—a remarkable experience that transports you back in time. It's a little bit like walking the old cobblestone roads of Europe.

It reminds me of places like Bath and Oxford, England, cities weathered by time and filled with memories. New Orleans is more than 300 years old, which means it's been around since before

America was even a country. A mix of Spanish and French influence is palpable in the French Quarter, the oldest part of the city.

We strolled from shop to shop, sipping coffee, and Joelle poured out her heart. She described in detail a fresh vision for her life. Through her own health journey, Joelle shed 20 pounds and gained authority over her relationship with food. She discovered new ways to master long-term food allergies, lower her blood pressure, and fuel her body in a way that was about living well.

It produced confidence, meaning, and purpose, and she ached to see others walk the same path. Joelle was all in to become a health coach. She planned to help create and build family legacies of health and she wanted it to start with us. As we meandered down Iberville Street, Joelle spoke passionately about breaking the chains that ensnared so much of America. Obesity, and its attendant diseases, doesn't need to be the norm in our country any longer.

I would be Joelle's first official client (read, guinea pig). She took on her new role with conviction and passion. Which was good, because for her to help me, she'd need to be on her A-game. It would deeply impact her for me to be successful because she loved me and wanted me healthy. The icing on the gluten-free cake? My success would also help her launch this new business.

She'd already helped so many people get healthy personally that it

My wife had a vision, and I faced a decision. I could sit on the sidelines and cheer her on, or I could jump into the game with her.

made sense to become an officially certified health coach. My wife had a vision, and I faced a decision. I could sit on the sidelines and cheer her on, or I could jump into the game with her.

In that moment I discovered one of the reasons I desperately wanted to win in my health. I found my WHY—and it was my internal fire burning fiercely for a reason beyond myself. If I failed, I wasn't just failing me. I was failing my wife in the area she wanted to win in—a new business with a mission to help thousands of people and their families get healthy.

I could see it burning in her eyes and hear it dripping from her words. She discovered a life calling and purpose, and I was determined not to work against her. This was a scoreboard moment. My wife wanted to grow, and this was a moment I could help her.

THE BLUE DOOR

In New Orleans, we lodged at the swanky Ritz-Carlton on the club level. This was not our normal landing pad and the luxuries overwhelmed us. For example, just to find our room, we were given a special key with instructions. We had to locate a specific elevator that would lead to a blue door.

Behind that blue door was magic.

This Ritz-Carlton offered every luxury and convenience, including access to delicious food and delicacies 24-hours a day, their chefs constantly on call. Need a créme brulee at 2 a.m.? No problem. Want a full tray of freshly-caught smoked salmon? Voila.

A bit thirsty? Simply grab a glass and pull a lever at the tap of hundred-dollar wines in the lounge.

Remember, I love food, and used it as a crutch to cope, celebrate, cure boredom, and deal with every other emotion. This situation was like an alcoholic in a liquor store where everything's free.

I faced an incredible challenge—stick to my health program or bail. In my previous life, I would've used this as an excuse to pick up my health program when we got home. However, my Life Scoreboard was set and I committed to a timeline. More so, I committed to my wife. Cheating wasn't an option.

And you know what? I did it.

I stuck to plan and even lost fat in New Orleans. The reason? Not only did I have a vivid Promised Land, I now had a tried and true WHY. I would rather die than fail my wife. Yours doesn't have to be that dramatic, but in my great struggle for health, I needed something with nuclear power I could tap into at will. My victory was also her victory; and my failure meant her failure. This is why I believe to accomplish your purpose, it will be intrinsically tied to other people.

Together, we win.

To improve the lives of people around you, it will mean a life of service and impact that goes beyond achieving your goals. When we win in these kinds of ways, we all win together. After all, ships rise together with the tide.

Together, we win.

FINDING YOUR WHY

No one has articulated the importance of finding your WHY better than the brilliant Simon Sinek. The framework he shares in *Find Your Why*[5], guides us to answer two questions:

- *What do you want to contribute to the world?*
- *What impact will this contribution make?*

It looks like this: **TO** [CONTRIBUTION] **SO THAT** [IMPACT].

For example, my WHY Statement went like this: **TO** achieve my healthy weight **SO THAT** my wife can fulfill her dream of health coaching.

As you saw with my Promised Land Statement, my WHY has deepened considerably. But this is the spark that set my heart ablaze. Now, try writing your own. Perfection isn't our goal—progress is. So find something that stokes your coals. I found my WHY in the French Quarter. Where will you find yours?

TO _____
                                      (contribution)

SO THAT_____
                                      (impact)

© SIMON SINEK, "FIND YOUR WHY"

---

[5] Sinek, Simon, et al. "Find Your Why: A Practical Guide for Discovering Purpose for You and Your Team." New York, New York, Portfolio/Penguin, 2017.

CHAPTER SEVEN:

CROSSING
THE STREAM

Step back on to the bank of the river and set your sights on the Promised Land. Let's hand-select stones to get you across. Each stone can be thought of as a goal. There are a million different methods for goal setting. If you have one that works for you, awesome, use it here.

If not, I'm going to introduce a new variation on something popularized in recent years by an author and genius named Michael Hyatt called SMART goals. We're going to adapt the acronym, and call our version SMRTY goals (sounds like "smarty"). These stand for Specific, Measurable, Relevant, Time-boxed, and Yours.

In the traditional SMART goal method, A stands for Achievable. But often I found when we try to craft goals that are achievable, we actually limit ourselves. What if Noah thought the Ark was too big and settled on a dingy? Or if David traded fighting Goliath head on for a diplomatic solution? Or if Winston Churchill decided taking down the Nazi regime was ludicrous, and tried to appease them instead?

Even a failed moonshot can get you into orbit. So, let's plan big.

I love a giant-filled Promised Land because, by the time you get across the stream, you're going to be a different person. A better person. Because that future version of you is capable of more than you ever thought possible.

So let's choose your stones. Here is my Promised Land Statement:

PROMISED LAND

> Today, I control food, it doesn't control me. I'm fit, bold, and ready to serve others. I feel confident, strong, and passionate about inspiring others to get healthy. My average day starts with wearing whatever I want and confidently growing my health. And I'm now the kind of person who isn't consumed with what others think of me.

And to achieve it, I'm going to spell out specific, measurable, relevant, and time-boxed goals. The power in this exercise is twofold:

1. A Dominican University study found that people who write down their goals are more likely to accomplish them[6].
2. Clarity is the greatest motivator.

SPECIFIC   MEASURABLE   RELEVANT   TIME-BOXED   YOURS

SPECIFIC

Each goal needs to be specific. For instance, if we're looking at health, my goal shouldn't be "to lose weight." If I lose half an ounce, I've already achieved it. Instead, my goal is to lose 35 pounds of fat and maintain 145 pounds of lean body mass.

Hone in, and get very practical and clear on exactly what steps you need to take to reach that goal. How to complete tasks that lead the way will be covered in the next chapter.

MEASURABLE

Once you've set a specific goal, make sure it's measurable. You want to know where you're at in relation to hitting that goal. It's sort of

[6] See Study Summary here: https://www.dominican.edu/academics/lae/undergraduate-programs/psych/faculty/assets-gail-matthews/researchsummary2.pdf

like depth perception. If you jump for a stone across a river, but it's actually further than you thought, you're going to get wet (maybe even swept away). Also, if it's closer than you thought, you might leap right over it.

You want to be able to measure your progress in relation from where you currently stand. As the great Peter Drucker said, "What gets measured gets managed."

Measurement also means you actively calculate progress in real time. Don't simply set a goal, wait for the date to arrive, and hope you hit it. A measurement system provides a feedback loop to check progress.

Three years ago, I started ghostwriting full time. My first contract included five books in a single month. That is an insane number of books, even in a year. To do it in a single month was overwhelming, but I didn't have another job and the golden opportunity to make money as a writer landed in my lap.

So, I signed on the dotted line and then an awful realization hit—I had no idea how to get it done. This is where measurements saved me. I used the same spreadsheet to track my progress toward my goal of having those books drafted.

I worked in short sprints of 25-minute writing sessions. I tracked my word count target and my actual word count, and eventually hit the count to finish the books on time. The last thing I did was take notes on how things went. It's the most methodical I have ever been in my life, and it worked.

Whether it's a spreadsheet, a tracking app, or just a simple note-book, find a form of measurement. It's your reality feedback loop to tell you if you are stepping on the stones. If you're not, measurements help you adjust. Do I need to hit the gas or can I afford to back off and and save my energy. Is this a sprint or a marathon?

The five books was a sprint, and as I tracked my progress I grew more efficient. One thing I realized was that sleep was crucial.

I also learned that every one hour of work between 5 a.m. and 10 a.m. is worth three hours of work anytime after 5 p.m. and that's a lesson that serves me to this day. The more I work at night, the less efficient, productive and happy I will be. My mind doesn't work great when the clock strikes midnight. So, I hit the pause button, turn in and get up early the next day.

My mental energy is at its all-time high during the day, between the hours of 5 a.m. and 10 a.m. It's why I generally avoid scheduling meetings during that window of time. I protect it for my most productive, brain-intensive tasks.

Measurement will serve you well, not just now, but moving into all your life areas.

Measurement will serve you well, not just now, but moving into all your life areas. It's a reality check— where are you growing and where do you need to grow? It's why every sports team worth its salt will keep stats.

Returning to the number-one scoreboard fans in history, baseball connoisseurs track hundreds of stats every game. In fact, there's a discipline called sabermetrics devoted to its scientific analysis. (Nerd alert.) One of America's greatest sportswriters once quipped, "Baseball fans pay more attention to numbers than CPAs."[7]

Measure your progress with the tenacity of a baseball fan.

RELEVANT

Next, let's talk about relevance. Your goals (or stepping stones) need to be relevant, not simply to the goal itself, but also to your WHY. It has to connect deeply and resonate with you. If you don't understand exactly why you're doing it, you will give up when it gets tough. When you are burning the midnight oil, you cling to something that's actually relevant to your goals.

Take my health journey, for instance. So many times I set goals of hitting the gym six days a week, or finishing P90x, Insanity, or some other crazy workout program. But deep inside I longed for confidence, self-mastery, and significance. Goals of a skinny waistline or reps in the gym weren't aligned with my real WHY— because I hadn't tapped into it yet.

Goals like those quickly became irrelevant. When I was so sore I could barely walk after a tough P90X session, or when I woke up and simply didn't feel like working out, I skipped out. Not much was on the line. If your goals aren't relevant to both the Promised Land *and* the reason why you're trying to get there in the first place, it's a recipe for failure.

---

[7] https://www.baseball-reference.com/bullpen/Sabermetrics

TIME-BOXED

Next, time-box your goals. This simply means a goal will be completed within a specific duration of time. This is key because it helps you set what I call your "aggression threshold."

The faster you want to achieve a high-level of growth, the more aggressive the effort. The easiest way to visualize the idea is to imagine three toggles. Think of them like knobs on a control panel, side-by-side, labeled: *growth, effort, and time.* Here's what each configuration looks like.

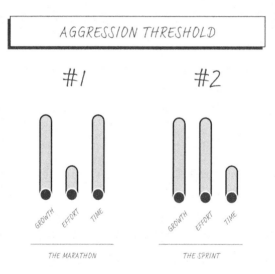

While there are many ways this could be visualized, let's keep it simple and break down the two most likely configurations.

#1. The Marathon: In this scenario, your growth goal is high. However, to avoid cranking up the intensity, you use a generous timeline. This means you'll achieve high growth in a longer time-box.

#2. The Sprint: In this scenario, your growth goal is high *and* you want results fast. This means your effort will be very intense in a shorter time-box.

When setting time-boxes, consider your aggression threshold. If you want big growth in a small time-box, get ready for some intense pain. Pain is worth it at the right time. I set huge goals in small time-boxes all the time, and let me tell you, it's not always worth it.

Let's take a real-life example. A friend prepared to set time goals on his Life Scoreboard. He initially set an aggressive savings goal that meant he needed to double his monthly salary. Was it possible? Yes. Would it hurt? Ouch. Ouch. Ouch.

During the time-boxing stage he realized the amount of extra work he'd have to take on would conflict with his wife's scoreboard. Kudos to him for paying attention.

The aggression threshold frames an incredible conversation around time allocation for couples, business partners, ministry teams, and anyone else trying to accomplish things together. Now, instead of dreaming up big goals with tiny timelines and then crashing off the rails, you possess a tool to intelligently set, plan for, and coordinate on goal accomplishment.

If you are married and both have different goals that require an insane amount of time, you may need to decide who is watching the kids at what time. Or, consider things like not watching so much Netflix or hanging out with friends.

On a personal level it's also important for you to look at other goals and commitments. Are you overextending yourself? (I often do.) Or, are you not challenging yourself? Do you have more fuel in the tank?

Your aggression threshold sets the pace for everything.

Your aggression threshold sets the pace for everything. It will make or break you. Get clear on how quickly you're going to accomplish things, and what it will take from both of you to play on the same team, win together, and still love each other in the end.

YOURS

Finally, we come to the Y in our SMRTY plan. The goal has to be yours! I know it seems obvious, but you don't want to be pursuing someone else's goal because you will never truly take ownership of it.

Is this genuinely your goal? Is it something you're passionate about? Or is it something people in your life would *like* you to be passionate about? You don't want to end up in someone else's Promised Land, so set goals that will carry you into *your* Promised Land. You could have every other component right, but if it's not yours, it often won't matter enough to stick it out.

BRING IT ALL TOGETHER

Big goals seem impossible—until we break them down into smaller steps. Let's break your Promised Land Statement down into a handful of SMRTY goals. I'll show you how it worked for me. And remember, your goals are the WHAT, not the HOW.

First, refer back to your Promised Land Statement. Here's mine:

PROMISED LAND

Today, I control food, it doesn't control me. I'm fit, bold, and ready to serve others. I feel confident, strong, and passionate about inspiring others to get healthy. My average day starts with wearing whatever I want and confidently growing my health. And I'm now the kind of person who isn't consumed with what others think of me.

This statement is loaded with all the feels. There are emotions, mental states, identity statements, and more. However, the fundamental goal that would help me unlock all this is achieving a healthy weight. When I started, I weighed 207.2 pounds at 30.1 percent body fat. That's a Dad bod at best, and a walking burrito at worst.

I did some research, talked to my genius wife, and made a plan[8]. Here are the key things I learned to set myself up for success:

- *My healthy weight is 165–175 pounds—or at least 32.2 pounds lighter. This became my Promised Land goal.*
- *Fat loss is the goal, not weight loss. I needed to maintain my lean body mass by eating enough protein and Grandma exercises (like walking).*

---

[8] These are MY goals for MY body and MY health situation. I consulted our doctor before starting this plan. You should too. This exercise is neither a promise for results nor professional medical advice. This is simply the structure I followed to un-fatten.

- *For visible abs (vain, I know), guys need to be around 12 percent body fat. I used inexpensive calipers to calculate my body current fat percentage, thus discovering I had about 18 percent to cut.*

- *For the most accurate results, I ordered a new scale. Then, I weighed myself each morning after peeing and before eating or drinking anything.*

- *Studies find weighing in daily results in more weight loss because it keeps you focused[9].*

- *I learned to calculate my basal metabolic rate (BMR) and total energy expenditure (TEE) to find my target daily calories and macronutrient intake (fat, protein, carbohydrates).*

- *I realized drinking at least half of my weight in clean water is critical for weight loss.*

- *I also found that sleeping 7–8 hours is paramount for a gajillion reasons[10]. Your body is producing hormones, healing itself, and setting you up for your healthy weight.*

Joelle understood all this, but getting personal clarity on what I needed to do and why was a linchpin for setting the right goals in proper time-boxes. With her coaching and my research, it was time to set my goals.

[9] VanWormer, Jeffrey J., et al. "The Impact of Regular Self-Weighing on Weight Management: A Systematic Literature Review." International Journal of Behavioral Nutrition and Physical Activity, vol. 5, no. 1, 2008, p. 54, ijbnpa.biomedcentral. com/articles/10.1186/1479-5868-5-54, 10.1186/1479-5868-5-54.

[10] Nedeltcheva, Arlet V., et al. "Insufficient Sleep Undermines Dietary Efforts to Reduce Adiposity." Annals of Internal Medicine, vol. 153, no. 7, 5 Oct. 2010, p. 435, annals.org/aim/article-abstract/746184/insufficient-sleep-undermines-dietary-efforts-reduce-adiposity, 10.7326/0003-4819-153-7-201010050-00006.

Your goals become the stones you'll use to cross the river into the Promised Land. My journey began in early September, and here's how I mapped out my goals.

GOALS	WHEN	POINTS
200 lbs @ 27.5% body fat	Sep 13	
190 lbs @ 23.7% body fat	Sep 27	
180 lbs @ 19.5% body fat	Oct 18	
172.5 lbs @ 16% body fat	Dec 1	
★ 165 lbs @ 12.2% body fat	Dec 31	

The star marks the goal in your Promised Land. We will address how the "Points" column works in the next chapter on scoring. But right now, notice the SMRTY structure of each goal:

- *Specific: exact weight and body fat percentage*
- *Measureable: I can know precisely how I'm doing*
- *Relevant: achieving each goal carries me to my Promised Land*
- *Time-boxed: I assigned a date for each goal, mapping out a 4-month fat loss journey*
- *Yours: I was all in on every goal and deeply connected with my WHY*

Now, you try. Break down your Promised Land Statement into SMRTY goals (but don't worry about the "Points" yet).

GOALS	WHEN	POINTS
★		

STILL ON THE JOURNEY

As I write this, I'm on track to reach my goal weight and body fat percentage by the December 31, 2019. I followed a structured eating plan and radically changed my food habits and mindset along the way. Honestly, I can't overstate how incredible this process has been. And because we've brought family and friends along with us, we've all won together.

I hear over and over again from our clients that weight loss is a catalyst for rewiring their brains. Part of this, I believe, is because it's been such a giant dark spot in their lives—like it was in mine. Because there has been deep pain, insecurity, and failure associated with battling the scale, all the shortcomings in other areas of our lives orbit around this one. Losing in this Life Area forms into a black hole, inescapable and defeating.

However, right when we start winning here, it unlocks nearly every other area. Why? Because step-by-step we're proving to ourselves we can slay the baddest giants in our personal growth.

Your Promised Land and goals may look totally different. Maybe you're paying off credit card debt, or starting a new business, ministry, or side-hustle. You might even be overcoming an addiction to pornography, shopping, or alcohol (in which case, I recommend seeking professional help as one of your goals).

No matter your goals, I believe winning in a place you've consistently lost for years will function in the same way: unlocking a path to growth in every other area of your life.

Now, I am still very much on the journey. I fight old habits, but I'm winning every day. The Promised Land is real, it's possible, and it's yours if you craft the path and walk it.

Last, if reaching your healthy weight is something you'd like help with, don't go it alone. Our incredibly inspiring community has made all the difference. As a thank you for getting this book, you can signup for a free 20-minute health assessment with Joelle and me. Schedule here: **rebrand.ly/free-health-assessment**

Now, let's break down your goals into the final step, your Point-Scoring Actions.

CHAPTER EIGHT:

HOW WE
SCORE

Growing up a fat kid had its fair share of troubles, but also some sneaky benefits. In sixth grade I played in a city-wide flag football league with 14 teams. We played every Saturday and it was an incredible amount of fun. The same Wolf Pack from school banded together as a team, only this time they didn't get the upper hand on me.

In the league, our team ended up winning the entire city championship, thanks to an innovative play affectionately called the Rollie Pollie.

I played center, or the guy who hikes the ball through his legs from the flattering squat position. I looked like the husky kid who'd operate at a glacial pace, but let me tell you, I moved like a ninja.

I could jet from one side of the field to the other faster than a rocket full of monkeys. In the Rollie Pollie, I hiked the ball to the quarterback, and rolled out to the right or the left. Thinking I was crazy, the other team would rush the quarterback to snatch his flag.

They disregarded the chubby kid, who by then was well on his way to scoring after the quarterback lobbed it over the mob coming toward him. The Rollie Pollie took us to victory nearly every game. It was our secret weapon.

Your Point-Scoring Actions (PSAs) function the same way. They are the key movements and plays that will put points on the board. They will come from consistent action and application.

THE SCORE TAKES CARE OF ITSELF

What plays do you need to make in order to put points on your scoreboard? How do you make measurable progress toward your goal? While these will often become habits, they begin as new actions that may be difficult at first, but require consistent follow-through.

This is where structure and organization pay extreme dividends for you. When I started my health program more than 30 pounds ago, my PSAs were simple: follow the playbook. That meant jumping into the structure of eating specific foods at specific times of the day, drinking more water, prioritizing sleep, decreasing stress, and exercising. My aggression threshold was set properly, not extreme. I just made necessary changes and stayed consistent.

In his classic book, *The Score Takes Care of Itself*, coach Bill Walsh calls this the "relentless execution of fundamentals." He identified the key basic elements his teams needed to execute every time, and the score took care of itself. When they identified these fundamental components that carried them to victory, they relentlessly executed against their competitors.

This is what you're doing here. You're building your playbook to take you from one stone to the next. Follow through, and the score will take care of itself. Organization is perhaps your greatest ally here. Structure your day, so you know exactly what you should be doing.

Here are my PSAs:

POINT-SCORING ACTIONS

EAT 6 SMALL MEALS DAILY, 2—3 HOURS APART
SLEEP 8 HOURS EVERY NIGHT
PELOTON 30 MINUTES 5 DAYS PER WEEK
TRACK PROGRESS IN JOURNAL AND SHARE WITH IT'S YOUR TIME TRIBE
READ "HABITS OF HEALTH" & USE "LIFE BOOK"

Structure your day, so you know exactly what you should be doing.

What is your Rollie Pollie? What works for you every time? When you outline your point-scoring activities, you will do so for each goal. So, every goal will have its own point-scoring action attached to it. You will time-box these as well. It might be daily, it might be weekly. It might even be one time.

Perhaps you need to schedule a doctor's appointment. Maybe you need to deposit your first $100 in a savings account. Maybe you need to talk to your spouse about a monthly date night. Maybe you need to clear the cabinets of foods that don't line up with your health goals. Maybe you need to put a limit on TV time. Maybe you need to set the alarm 30 minutes earlier every day to get up and write that book. Maybe it's time to develop that devotional habit, finding a place, time, and plan to study the Bible and pray.

(You can also receive Gospel-centered, Bible-based devotions sent to your inbox free every day by visiting ShortDailyDevotions. com).

Whatever your PSAs, list them in the order and the frequency they need to happen. This is where the rubber meets the road. Let me be clear. There are no magic pills, and no silver bullets. This is not a system of shortcuts. It's a system of focus. It's a system of consistency. Do the work on a system of accountability.

It's your turn. Add your PSAs.

POINT-SCORING ACTIONS

TIME TO SCORE

The three related components to winning include: your points, your score, and your PSAs. Your PSAs are the playbook. Your "Points" column tallies how many points you've scored toward your Promised Land Goal (the one with the star). And your score, on the top right, is a reflection of total progress toward winning here. One hundred points wins the game.

Here's a snapshot of my scoreboard right now.

AREA

HEALTHY BODY WEIGHT

SCORE

70 / 100

PROMISED LAND

Today, I control food, it doesn't control me. I'm fit, bold, and ready to serve others. I feel confident, strong, and passionate about inspiring others to get healthy. My average day starts with wearing whatever I want and confidently growing my health. And I'm now the kind of person who isn't consumed with what others think of me.

GOALS

GOALS	WHEN	POINTS
~~200 lbs @ 27.5% body fat~~	Sep 13	20
~~190 lbs @ 23.7% body fat~~	Sep 27	15
~~180 lbs @ 19.5% body fat~~	Oct 18	15
~~172.5 lbs @ 16% body fat~~	Dec 1	20
★ 165 lbs @ 12.2% body fat	Dec 31	30

POINT-SCORING ACTIONS

EAT 6 SMALL MEALS DAILY, 2–3 HOURS APART

SLEEP 8 HOURS EVERY NIGHT

PELOTON 30 MINUTES 5 DAYS PER WEEK

TRACK PROGRESS IN JOURNAL AND SHARE WITH IT'S YOUR TIME TRIBE

READ "HABITS OF HEALTH" & USE "LIFE BOOK"

We've already covered your PSAs, so let's finish out your scoreboard with the Points and Score sections.

POINTS

Your points are super simple. Assign each goal a point value based on how hard you think it'll be to achieve. It isn't scientific, but it works. The sum of the points should be 100. And each time you accomplish a goal, add the number of points to your score.

SCORE

Right now, I'm at 70/100 points. This is still a huge victory. It's the lowest weight I've been at since high school. Eleven years later, and I weigh less than I did on my wedding day, all while maintaining my muscle mass. I celebrate and savor each win because I've done the hard work. I watched my progress as I worked my playbook, walked out my PSAs and achieved each goal. By December 31, it's happy-dance time in my Promised Land.

I've done this in other life areas, as well; including this book. Today, it's simply how I get things done. When I get to one Promised Land, I create another. It's a way to avoid the stagnant waters of a life with no goals and no way to move forward.

If you feel overwhelmed by a goal—because the Promised Land is not a few leaps away, but a few miles—don't be shaken. Feeling overwhelmed is a signal you may want to break down your goals into even smaller components. Use these steps and your progress

Let success become a moving target for you. will take you from one rock to the next until you get there.

If you are too scared to create a Promised Land and work toward it, it means you stop growing and stay put. Let success become a moving target for you. Revise your playbook, build new skills, learn about yourself and sharpen the areas of your life that have been dulled by a cycle of bad habits.

Above all, keep your eyes on that Promised Land. Clarity is the greatest motivator. Keep jumping.

CHAPTER NINE:

THE REAL SILVER BULLET

Several years ago I drove a pewter gray minivan I affectionately nicknamed the Silver Bullet. One day, I was cruising somewhere with my oldest daughter Fallon, a toddler at the time, when the Silver Bullet lurched, seized, sputtered, and then died—in the middle of an intersection during the South Dakota winter, of course. To make matters worse, the sliding door next to Fallon's car seat started opening and closing by itself.

So there I am, pushing my caput van out of a busy intersection with the side door next to my screaming two-year-old opening and closing like a clown car. Honest to goodness, a lady pulled up alongside of us and visibly gaped at the side door, revealing a tiny blonde girl yelling, "Cold!" We were a spectacle. My thighs burned as I pushed my mechanical warhorse into a gas station parking lot.

The Silver Bullet died that day—and for many of us, so do systems like the Life Scoreboard. We're excited, know where we're going, and start off with a bang until the inevitable obstacle happens. Our Silver Bullet plan dies in the middle of a busy intersection.

It could be that we get sick or injured on a workout program, then hang up our gym clothes on the unused treadmill in our basement. Defeated again. Or perhaps we binge on some pizza, nachos, candy, popcorn, and a cocktail on a Friday night out with friends, thinking, *I'll get back on track Monday*. Only, we never do. Weeks turn into months and our Silver Bullet of a system has become a dusty relic on the shelf.

Those are surface-level examples that throw us off time and again. But I also know life will bring more grisly foes to bear. Loved ones pass away and we bury our grief in food. We lose a job and the credit card bill skyrockets. Our spouse commits adultery and all of our supposed marital progress goes up in flames.

Life is not easy. We both know that. But I'm inviting you beyond the Silver Bullet mentality. This system won't work without you. There will be many "good" reasons to quit, to start over on Monday, to wait until next year.

My friend, you haven't made it this far to quit when giants come down the mountain to slay you.

My friend, you haven't made it this far to quit when giants come down the mountain to slay you. This is the season you change. This is the plan that works. It's your time. In this final chapter, I want to leave you with concrete concepts, inspiration to persevere, and science-backed proof you can do this.

DECISION POINT

Every great endeavor begins with a decision—*but not the kind we've come to know.* Decision comes from two Latin words *de-caedere*, and literally translated means "to cut off." This word means finality. It means a cutting off of all other paths, choices, or avenues. To say "yes" for real means every other option is killed.

Much like the call to discipleship, deciding to grow means no matter what, you will not quit. You might adjust. You might course correct mid-flight, but there will be no pooping out like my van in the intersection.

In the Army, there's a legendary document called the *12 Week Ranger Assessment and Selection Program Training Plan* (RASP).[11] They are phenomenal at understanding people. Here's how the guide begins:

Nothing is magic about this program. What will make this program work is you. Commit mentally to success and follow through with dedication and hard work. Although your muscles will eventually reach failure, never let your mind reach failure. Do not quit and approach this program and RASP with a fearless tenacity to go above and beyond the accepted "norm". If you are happy being ordinary, don't waste your/our time and stop reading now and go enjoy your life. If not, continue on relentlessly...

---

[11] Read the full guide here: https://rebrand.ly/ranger-training-guide

40 PERCENT RULE

I've returned to that introduction for motivation more times than I can count in the last several years. It's proven true every time I decided to continue on relentlessly. And I've come to learn, there is science at work, too.

A 2008 study demonstrates that when our minds believe we can achieve something, we're capable of more[12]. Researchers split subjects into two groups. Group A was given a high dose of caffeine, then performed a measured workout. Group B was given placebos, but told the pills were packed with a high dose of caffeine. Unbelievably, the placebo effect in Group B was larger, with a "significant increase in muscle work and decrease in perceived muscle fatigue." That's right, the placebo group lifted more weight while being less tired than the group pumped with caffeine.

When we think we're done, we've only reached 40 percent of our capabilities.

Navy SEALs call this phenomenon the "40 Percent Rule." When we think we're done, we've only reached 40 percent of our capabilities. Author and entrepreneur Jesse Itzler wrote about it in his book, *Living with a SEAL*. Jesse invited a Navy SEAL to come live with him, push him, and teach him to step out of his comfort zone.

[12] Pollo, Antonella, et al. "The Top-down Influence of Ergogenic Placebos on Muscle Work and Fatigue." European Journal of Neuroscience, vol. 28, no. 2, July 2008, pp. 379–388, 10.1111/j.1460-9568.2008.06344.x. Accessed 14 Dec. 2019.

On their first day together, the SEAL asked him to do as many pull-ups as he could. Jesse did eight. Then the SEAL told him to rest for 30 seconds, then try again. He did six. Then again. He did three. And then the SEAL told him, "We're not leaving until you do 100."

Even though he thought there was no way on earth he could do it, he pulled it off. One at a time, with little breaks in between. In an interview, Jesse said of this moment, "He showed me, proved to me...we're all capable of so much more than we think we are."[13]

CHOOSE YOUR HARD

Have you ever thought about how hard life is, no matter what? The real trick isn't found in chasing comfort or avoiding tough things. Instead, it's about choosing your hard. In my health, it was hard to get winded walking up stairs, burn with acid reflux, be embarrassed to take my shirt off, and find myself dominated by food. Honestly, I hated living like that. *It was hard.*

At the same time, following my Life Scoreboard has also been hard. I made new decisions, and change is difficult. I said no to things I wanted to eat. I exercised instead of vegging out. I invested money in the right food and supplements. I chose my hard. One led to life as I knew it and one led to health, or my Promised Land.

---

[13] Finch, Sidd. "The 40% Rule: A Navy SEAL's Secret to Mental Toughness." The Hustle, Dec. 2015, thehustle.co/40-percent-rule-navy-seal-secret-mental-toughness.

I'm 100 percent convinced I will achieve what I set out to do. Not because I'm a genius, but because I'm finally willing to commit.

Change will be hard, but it will be worth it. Comfort and your Promised Land are not the same thing. It's hard because it requires discomfort. No one knew this better than Jesus.

NEW WINESKINS

In Luke 5, people were confused. They wanted to know why Jesus and the disciples weren't fasting like the Pharisees and the disciples of John the Baptist. Everyone had an expectation that Jesus would maintain their vision for holiness and piety. Then he broke their expectations by living to standards of his own and his Father's:

> *He also told them a parable: "No one tears a piece from a new garment and puts it on an old garment. If he does, he will tear the new, and the piece from the new will not match the old. And no one puts new wine into old wineskins. If he does, the new wine will burst the skins and it will be spilled, and the skins will be destroyed. But new wine must be put into fresh wineskins. And no one after drinking old wine desires new, for he says, 'The old is good.'"* (Luke 5:36–39 ESV)

Disrupting the status quo meant life as people knew it changed.

God was doing a new thing (new wine). And this new thing required new behaviors (new wineskins). Disrupting the *status quo* meant life as people knew it changed. People projected their version of the Promised Land onto Jesus and his ministry.

They didn't like how he did things. Healing people on the Sabbath ruffled their feathers. And don't even get them started on the prostitutes and tax collectors He hung around!

Jesus explained if he tried to work God's plan in their ways, it would damage and tear apart the entire rescue mission. The garments would tear, the skins would burst, and no one would be saved. Despite this truth, people still loved the old ways of doing things—and because they clung to those old ways, they reaped the old results.

We cannot afford to be those people, clinging to the past, clinging to our comfort, saying things like, "Well, we've always done it this way..." Or, "If it ain't broke, don't fix it..." New results require new behaviors. Period.

If Jesus lived the life people expected, it would have devastated the whole world. Thankfully, he pursued his purpose undeterred. Because of this:

- His family didn't understand him (Mark 3:35).
- His hometown rejected him (Mark 6:3).
- Thousands of followers left him because he said hard things (John 6:66).
- His culture's leaders plotted to kill him and his friends (John 12:9–11).
- He was put to death on the cross (John 19:18).

Jesus was a disrupter who faithfully did and said only what the Father told him to (John 12:49). He maintained a single purpose.

His actions were relentlessly consistent and His aggression threshold was high. After all, he only had three years to save the world.

By accomplishing his mission—to seek and save the lost, bear witness to the truth, and be sacrificed as our substitute—Jesus saved the world. He fought the very forces of death and Hell on the open battlefield—and won.

TODAY WE WIN

I'm so passionate about this message because it's a repeating pattern: *fulfilling our purpose positively impacts the world.* It is transformative because it requires that we must grow to the measure of impact we make. The truth is, the only silver bullet that won't fail you is your relentless execution of the fundamentals of the playbook.

Align your efforts to win with (and for) the people around you. That means you don't begin this journey alone. Travel with as many people as you can. One of my favorite sayings is to "always learn for two." Your goal is to teach everything you've learned. To multiply the knowledge, strategies, and tactics entrusted to you.

We were created to win together.

Find people in your life who travel where you are—toward growth. The first thing God said wasn't good for man, was to be alone (Genesis 2:18). We are made for community. We are built to run alongside one another. We were created to win together.

To this point in my life, I haven't done community very well. I consistently battle fear and pride. Fear whispers, *No one will accept you...* And pride smugly declares, *You don't need anyone else...*

Today, that is changing. My Silver Bullet sputtered out and I was left in the intersection alone. I plugged into a vibrant community and learned you don't have to push on your own—and you shouldn't.

This is my hope for you, that no matter where you are in life—the Peach on the playground, or the victor hopping from Promised Land to Promised Land—you embrace your worth, your purpose, and your value to those around you.

Fundamentally, our significance is based on the impact we make in other people's lives. And this is a simple system to achieve what matters most in this world. Find your team, and let's win together. See you at the finish line.

EXERCISES:
YOUR LIFE SCOREBOARD

In this section, you will find every Life Scoreboard template in order. You can also download a free printable version by visiting:

rebrand.ly/life-scoreboard-workbook

*TELL ME ABOUT A TIME IN YOUR LIFE YOU FELT
LIKE YOU WERE WINNING?*

WHY?

WHY?

WHY?

WHY?

WHY?

*TELL ME ABOUT A TIME IN YOUR LIFE YOU FELT
LIKE YOU WERE LOSING?*

WHY?

WHY?

WHY?

WHY?

WHY?

WHAT LIFE AREAS WOULD YOU LIKE
TO GROW EXPONENTIALLY?

LIFE AREAS
BRAINSTORM

PRIORITIZE 3—5 LIFE AREAS FOR THE NEXT 90 DAYS

#1. _____

#2. _____

#3. _____

#4. _____

#5. _____

YOUR PROMISED LAND

	TODAY	FUTURE
HAVE		
FEEL		
AVG. DAY		
IDENTITY		

PROMISED LAND STATEMENT

TODAY, I _____

I FEEL _____

MY AVG. DAY _____

AND I'M THE KIND OF PERSON WHO _____

TO _____
                        (contribution)

SO THAT _____
                        (impact)

© SIMON SINEK, "FIND YOUR WHY"

S   **M**   **R**   **T**   **Y**

SPECIFIC   MEASURABLE   RELEVANT   TIME-BOXED   YOURS

AGGRESSION THRESHOLD

#1   #2

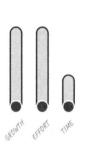

GROWTH EFFORT TIME   GROWTH EFFORT TIME

THE MARATHON   THE SPRINT

AREA

SCORE

/ 100

PROMISED LAND

GOALS	WHEN	POINTS
★		

POINT-SCORING ACTIONS

ACKNOWLEDGMENTS

If you've made it this far, I'll let you in on a little secret. I booked the venue to launch this book before I was done writing it. This gave me a little over one month to hustle through the 1,001 steps it takes to publish a great book. Normally, that'd be pretty scary. However, I had absolute confidence it would happen because of the people I'm about to thank.

If I've learned anything this year, it's that you can multiply your impact tenfold when you have the right team. And I have that team.

First, nothing in my life would be possible without Joelle, my wife and best friend. You've inspired, encouraged, and worked your tail off to help me—*and everyone else in your life*—win. When I don't get the chance to deeply connect with you every day, I feel it. My world starts spinning and I want to quit everything, until you hug me, ask me questions, and gently laugh at my drama. I love you and the new story we're writing together.

To Fallon, Kindy, and Wilder, my favorite individuals and noisy interns. Daddy loves you, and some day when you read this book (or don't, because your Dad wrote it so it's not that cool), I hope you see how much Mommy and I love you. You're proof that Psalm 127:3 is true. Also, please eat without us having to ask 576 times. (XOXO)

To our Haidle and Loftis family, for tirelessly stepping in with the kids and all of the life things that fall through the cracks! You've supported us in every way possible, and I hope you know the impact this project makes belongs to you, as well.

To my editor, Kayla Gahagan, for exhausting all of your red ink to make this book 1,000 times better than when it started. Your dedication and input is invaluable. You are a joy to work with and always come through. Thank the Lord for people like you who meet deadlines.

To my assistant and second-mind, Anna Thompson, for keeping the engine running and all of the cats herded. I'm so grateful you've brought your many talents to our team. I don't want to imagine Story Chorus without you. Plus, I'm still convinced you could run most of the world in 25 hours per week.

To our photographer extraordinaire, Lea Black, for showing the world how beautiful Joelle is and somehow making me look presentable. Our smiles are real because of your infectious joy. And my oh my, you are the best at what you do.

To my friends: Luke Torgerson, for listening to all of my crazy ideas on airplane rides. Doug and Thea Wood, for helping set this year into motion—this book would not have happened without your influence. Rohn Gibson, for helping this little birdy jump out of the nest. And Jeremy Brown, for teaching me how to make books.

Finally, to all of my Story Chorus team: Joelle, Anna, Kayla, Kathryn, Luke, and Remmington. We've only just begun.

ABOUT *the* AUTHOR

Jordan Loftis wears many hats.

He's a bestselling author, speaker, entrepreneur, Bible teacher, podcast host, pastor, father of three (Fallon, Kindy, Wilder), lucky husband of one (Joelle), and certified health coach.

His writing, resources, and videos focus on Christian living, self-improvement, and storytelling. And his work has appeared in publications like *Inc., Forbes, Entrepreneur, Adweek,* and *The Gospel Coalition.*

As founder of Story Chorus, Jordan leads a brilliant team to produce bestselling books and authoritative media platforms for leaders. His work in academia and ministry reaches hundreds of thousands of people in over 100 countries each year. And as the cofounder of It's Your Time Wellness with Joelle, his wife, he coaches people to achieve healthy minds, bodies, and spirits.

When he finally invents a time machine, he'll start some other companies and ministries. But for now, he's having the time of his life working closely with an incredible team, his stunning wife, and his family.

Jordan lives with his wife and kids in Bismarck, North Dakota.

loftis.co

storychorus.com

iytwellness.com

shortdailydevotions.com

•••

⊙ | @jordanloftiswrites

🖪 | /jordanloftiswrites

Made in the USA
Coppell, TX
31 January 2020